Chain-Free Crochet
Made Easy™

EDITED BY
JUDY CROW

HOUSE of
WHITE
BIRCHES
PUBLISHERS
SINCE 1947

Chain-Free Crochet Made Easy

EDITOR Judy Crow
ART DIRECTOR Brad Snow
PUBLISHING SERVICES DIRECTOR Brenda Gallmeyer

MANAGING EDITOR Carol Alexander
ASSISTANT ART DIRECTOR Nick Pierce
COPY SUPERVISOR Michelle Beck
COPY EDITORS Amanda Ladig, Susanna Tobias
TECHNICAL EDITOR Agnes Russell
TECHNICAL ARTIST Nicole Gage

GRAPHIC ARTS SUPERVISOR Ronda Bechinski
GRAPHIC ARTISTS Jessi Butler, Minette Collins Smith
PRODUCTION ASSISTANTS Marj Morgan, Judy Neuenschwander

PHOTOGRAPHY SUPERVISOR Tammy Christian
PHOTOGRAPHY Scott Campbell
PHOTO STYLIST Martha Coquat

Printed in China
First Printing: 2009
Library of Congress Control Number: 2008923207

Hardcover ISBN: 978-1-59217-225-2
Softcover ISBN: 978-1-59217-226-9

DRGbooks.com

1 2 3 4 5 6 7 8 9

Introduction

The daunting task of starting a chain has been eliminated with the marvelous chain-free method.

Imagine a technique that allows you to make the foundation chain and the stitches of the first row at the same time! Called foundation stitches, this little-known technique is easy and fun to do, allowing you to work exactly the number of stitches needed for the first row of your pattern.

In *Chain-Free Crochet Made Easy* we have made it easy and fun to learn by including step-by-step instructions, lots of color photos and illustrations on how to start chain-free projects using a single, double, half double and slip ring foundation. The basic idea for all foundation stitches is the same; once you understand the idea behind it, you will be able to work any stitch with ease.

You will find a wide variety of designs for you to choose from ranging from doilies to afghans, women's and men's sweaters, adorable baby booties, dresses and blankets, plus lots of other great to items for the home, gifts, fashions and Baby. You will see that no matter what design you choose to make, you can begin them all with the chain-free foundation.

Get stitching today!

Contents

Fabulous Fashions

Chapter Contents

Fashion Tunic

BY **TAMMY HILDEBRAND**

SKILL LEVEL
EXPERIENCED

FINISHED SIZES
Instructions given fit 32–34-inch bust *(small)*; changes for 36–38-inch bust *(medium)*, 40–42-inch bust *(large)* and 46–48-inch bust *(X-large)* are in [ ].

FINISHED GARMENT MEASUREMENTS
Bust: 34¾ inches *(small)*, [40 inches *(medium)*, 45¼ inches *(large)* and 50½ inches *(X-large)*]

Length: 28 inches *(small)*, [28 inches *(medium)*, 30 inches *(large)* and 30 inches *(X-large)*]

MATERIALS
• J&P Coats Royale Fashion Crochet size 3 crochet cotton (150 yds per ball): 12 [13, 14, 15] balls #226 natural
• Size E/4/3.5mm crochet hook or size needed to obtain gauge
• Tapestry needle
• 4 [4, 5, 5] gold 19mm decorative rose shank buttons

GAUGE
[Sc, ch 3, sk next 3 sts, (cl, ch 2, cl)] twice, sc, ch 3, cl OR [(sc, ch 3, sc), (2 tr, ch 3, 2 tr)] twice (sc, ch 3, sc) 2 tr = 4 inches

PATTERN NOTES
Weave in loose ends as work progresses.

Join rounds with slip stitch unless otherwise stated.

Tunic is started at the neck and worked down with left and right fronts and back worked separately to waist. At top of waist, tunic is worked in rounds. Sleeves and button bands are added later.

SPECIAL STITCHES
Beginning cluster (beg cl): Ch 3, insert hook in indicated st or sp, draw up a lp, yo, draw through 2 lps on hook, yo, insert hook in same st or sp and draw up a lp, yo, draw through 2 lps on hook, yo, draw through all 3 lps on hook.

Cluster (cl): Yo, insert hook in indicated st or sp, draw up a lp, yo, draw through 2 lps on hook, [yo, insert hook in same st, draw up a lp, yo, draw through 2 lps on hook] twice, yo, draw through all 4 lps on hook.

INSTRUCTIONS

YOKE
Foundation row: Starting at neckline edge, work **sc foundation st** *(see Foundation Stitches on page 172)* 155 [163, 171, 179] times, turn. *(155 [163, 171, 179] sc)*

Row 1 (WS): Ch 3 *(counts as first dc)*, (**cl**—*see Special Stitches*, ch 2, cl) in next st, [ch 3, sk next 3 sts, sc in next st, ch 3, sk next 3 sts, (cl, ch 2, cl) in next st] across to last st, dc in last st, turn. *(19 [20, 21, 22] sc, 2 dc, 40 [42, 44, 46] cl)*

LEFT FRONT
Row 1: Ch 1, sc in first st, [(sc, ch 3, sc) in next ch-2 sp, (2 tr, ch 3, 2 tr) in next sc] 3 [4, 5, 6] times, turn, leaving rem sts unworked. *(7 [9, 11, 13] sc, 12 [16, 20, 24] tr)*

Row 2: Ch 1, sc in first st, sc in next ch-3 sp, [ch 3, (cl, ch 2, cl) in next ch-3 sp, ch 3, sc in next ch-3 sp] 3 times, ch 3, (cl, ch 2, cl) in next ch-3 sp, dc in last st, turn. *(4 [4, 6, 7] sc, 1 dc, 6 [8, 10, 12] cl)*

Row 3: Ch 1, sc in first st, (sc, ch 3, sc) in next ch-2 sp, [(2 tr, ch 3, 2 tr) in next sc, (sc, ch 3, sc) in next ch-2 sp] across, (dc, ch 1, dc) in last st, turn. *(6 [8, 10, 12] sc, 3 dc, 12 [16, 20, 24] tr)*

Row 4: Ch 3, (cl, ch 2, cl) in next ch-1 sp, ch 3, sc in next ch-3 sp, ch 3, [(cl, ch 2, cl) in next ch-3

sp, ch 3, sc in next ch-3 sp, ch 3] up to last ch-3 sp, (cl, ch 2, cl) in ch-3 sp, dc in last st, turn. *(3 [4, 5, 6] sc, 2 dc, 8 [10, 12, 14] cl)*

Row 5: Ch 1, sc in first st, (sc, ch 3, sc) in next ch-2 sp, [(2 tr, ch 3, 2 tr) in next sc, (sc, ch 3, sc) in next ch-2 sp] across, sc in last st, turn. *(10 [12, 14, 16] sc, 12 [16, 20, 24] tr)*

Row 6: Ch 3, (cl, ch 2, cl) in next ch-3 sp, [ch 3, sc in next ch-3 sp, ch 3, (cl, ch 2, cl) in next ch-3 sp] across, dc in last st, turn. *(3 [4, 5, 6] sc, 2 dc, 8 [10, 12, 14] cl)*

Rows 7–18: [Rep rows 5 and 6 alternately] 6 times.

Row 19: Rep row 5, fasten off.

BACK
Row 1: For first armhole, sk next 4 cl and sc, join cotton with sl st in next sc, ch 4 *(counts as first tr)*, (tr, ch 2, 2 tr) in same sp, [(sc, ch 3, sc) in next ch-2 sp, (2 tr, ch 3, 2 tr) in next sc] 8 [9, 10, 11] times, turn, leaving rem sts unworked. *(16 [18, 20, 22] sc, 36 [40, 44, 48] tr)*

Row 2: Ch 1, sc in first st, sc in next ch-3 sp, [ch 3, (cl, ch 2, cl) in next ch-3 sp, ch 3, sc in next ch-3 sp] across, sc in last st, turn. *(11 [12, 13, 14] sc, 16 [18, 20, 22] cl)*

Row 3: Ch 4 *(counts as first dc, ch-1)*, dc in same sp, (2 tr, ch 3, 2 tr) in next sc, [sc in next ch-2 sp, (2 tr, ch 3, 2 tr) in next sc] across, (dc, ch 1, dc) in last st, turn. *(16 [18, 20, 22] sc, 4 dc, 36 [40, 44, 48] tr)*

Row 4: Ch 3, (cl, ch 2, cl) in next ch-1 sp, ch 3, sc in next ch-3 sp, ch 3, [(cl, ch 2, cl) in next ch-3 sp, ch 3, sc in next ch-3 sp, ch 3] up to ch-1 sp, (cl, ch 2, cl) in next ch-1 sp, dc in 3rd ch of beg ch-4, turn. *(9 [10, 11, 12] sc, 2 dc, 20 [22, 24, 26] cl)*

Row 5: Ch 1, sc in first st, (sc, ch 3, sc) in next ch-2 sp, [(2 tr, ch 3, 2 tr) in next sc, (sc, ch 3, sc) in next ch-2 sp] across, sc in last st, turn. *(22 [24, 26, 28] sc, 36 [40, 44, 48] tr)*

Row 6: Ch 3, (cl, ch 2, cl) in next ch-3 sp, [ch 3, sc in next ch-3 sp, ch 3, (cl, ch 2, cl) in next ch-3 sp] across, dc in last st, turn.

Rows 7–18: [Rep rows 5 and 6 alternately] 6 times, turn.

Row 19: Rep row 5, fasten off.

RIGHT FRONT
Row 1: For 2nd armhole, sk next 4 cl and sc, join cotton with sl st in next sc, ch 4, (tr, ch 2, 2 tr) in same sp, [(sc, ch 3, sc) in next ch-2 sp, (2 tr, ch 3, 2 tr) in next sc] across, turn.

Row 2: Ch 1, sc in first st, sc in next ch-3 sp, [ch 3, (cl, ch 2, cl) in next ch-3 sp, ch 3, sc in next ch-3 sp] across, sc in last st, turn.

Row 3: Ch 4, (sc, ch 3, sc) in next ch-2 sp, [(2 tr, ch 3, 2 tr) in next sc, (sc, ch 3, sc) in next ch-2 sp] across, sc in last st, turn.

Row 4: Ch 3, (cl, ch 2, cl) in next ch-3 sp, ch 3, [sc in next ch-3 sp, ch 3, (cl, ch 2, cl) in next ch-3 sp, ch 3] across, (cl, ch 2, cl) in ch-1

sp, dc in 3rd ch of ch-4, turn.

Row 5: Ch 1, sc in first st, (sc, ch 3, sc) in next ch-2 sp, [(2 tr, ch 3, 2 tr) in next sc, (sc, ch 3, sc) in next ch-2 sp] across, sc in last st, turn.

Row 6: Ch 3, (cl, ch 2, cl) in next ch-3 sp, [ch 3, sc in next ch-3 sp, ch 3, (cl, ch 2, cl) in next ch-3 sp] across, dc in last st, turn.

Rows 7–18: [Rep rows 5 and 6 alternately] 6 times, turn.

Row 19: Rep row 5, **do not fasten off**.

BODY
Row 1: Ch 3, (cl, ch 2, cl) in next ch-3 sp, [ch 3, sc in next ch-3 sp, ch 3, (cl, ch 2, cl) in next ch-3 sp] across, dc in last st, working in sts across Back, dc in first st, (cl, ch 2, cl) in next ch-3 sp, [ch 3, sc in next ch-3 sp, ch 3, (cl, ch 2, cl) in next ch-3 sp] across, dc in last st, working in sts across Right Front, dc in first st, (cl, ch 2, cl) in next ch-3 sp, [ch 3, sc in next ch-3 sp, ch 3, (cl, ch 2, cl) in next ch-3 sp] across, dc in last st, turn. *(15 [18, 21, 24] sc, 6 dc, 36 [42, 48, 54] cl)*

Row 2: Ch 1, sc in first st, *(sc, ch 3, sc) in next ch-2 sp, [(2 tr, ch 3, 2 tr) in next sc, (sc, ch 3, sc) in next ch-2 sp] up to joining, (2 tr, ch 3, 2 tr) in center of underarm, rep from *, (sc, ch 3, sc) in next ch-2 sp, [(2 tr, ch 3, 2 tr) in next sc, (sc, ch 3, sc) in next ch-2 sp] to end, sc in last st, turn.

Row 3: Ch 3, (cl, ch 2, cl) in next

ch-3 sp, [ch 3, sc in next ch-3 sp, (cl, ch 2, cl) in next ch-3 sp] across, dc in last st, turn. *(17 [20, 23, 26] sc, 2 dc, 36 [42, 48, 54] cl)*

Row 4: Ch 1, sc in first sc, (sc, ch 3, sc) in next ch-2 sp, [(2 tr, ch 3, 2 tr) in next sc, (sc, ch 3, sc) in next ch-2 sp] across, sc in last st, turn.

Sizes Large & X-Large Only
Rows 5–8: Rep rows 3 and 4.

All Sizes
Rnd 1: Now working in rnds, ch 3, (cl, ch 2, cl) in next ch-3 sp, [ch 3, sc in next ch-3 sp, ch 3, (cl, ch 2, cl) in next ch-3 sp] across, ch 3, **join** *(see Pattern Notes)* in 3rd ch of beg ch-3.

Rnd 2: Sl st in each of next 2 chs, ch 1, sc in same sp, (sc, ch 3, sc) in next ch-2 sp, [(2 tr, ch 3, 2 tr) in next sc, (sc, ch 3, sc) in next ch-2 sp] around, join in first sc, turn.

Rnd 3: Ch 1, sc in same st as joining, ch 1, (cl, ch 2, cl) in next ch-3 sp, ch 1, [sc in next ch-3 sp, ch 1, (cl, ch 2, cl) in next ch-3 sp, ch 1] around, join in first sc, turn.

Rnd 4: Sl st in each st to next ch-2 sp, ch 1, (sc, ch 1, sc) in same sp, (2 tr, ch 1, 2 tr) in next sc, [(sc, ch 1, sc) in next ch-2 sp, (2 tr, ch 1, 2 tr) in next sc] around, join in first sc, turn.

Rnd 5: Sl st in each st to next ch-1 sp, ch 1, sc in same sp, ch 1, (cl, ch 2, cl) in next ch-1 sp, ch 1, [sc in next ch-1 sp, ch 1, (cl, ch 2, cl) in next ch-1 sp, ch 1]

around, join in first sc, turn.

Rnds 6–9: [Rep rnds 4 and 5 alternately] twice.

Rnd 10: Sl st in each st to next ch-2 sp, ch 1, (sc, ch 2, sc) in same sp, (2 tr, ch 2, 2 tr) in next sc, [(sc, ch 2, sc) in next ch-2 sp, (2 tr, ch 2, 2 tr) in next sc] around, join in first sc, turn.

Rnd 11: Sl st in each st to next ch-1 sp, ch 1, sc in same sp, ch 2, (cl, ch 2, cl) in next ch-2 sp, ch 2, [sc in next ch-2 sp, ch 2, (cl, ch 2, cl) in next ch-2 sp, ch 2] around, join in first sc, turn.

Rnd 12: Sl st in each st to next ch-2 sp, ch 1, (sc, ch 3, sc) in same sp, (2 tr, ch 3, 2 tr) in next sc, [(sc, ch 3, sc) in next ch-2 sp, (2 tr, ch 3, 2 tr) in next sc] around, join in first sc, turn.

Rnd 13: Sl st in each st to next ch-3 sp, ch 1, sc in same sp, ch 3, (cl, ch 2, cl) in next ch-3 sp, ch 3, [sc in next ch-3 sp, ch 3, (cl, ch 2, cl) in next ch-3 sp, ch 3] around, join in first sc, turn.

Rnds 14–21: [Rep rnds 12 and 13 alternately] 4 times.

Rnd 22: Rep rnd 12.

Rnd 23: Sl st in each st to next ch-3 sp, ch 1, sc in same sp, ch 3, [(cl, ch 2, cl) in next ch-3 sp, ch 3, sc in next ch-3 sp, ch 3] 1 [2, 3, 4] time(s), (cl, ch 2) twice and cl in next ch-3 sp, ch 3, sc in next ch-3 sp, ch 3, [(cl, ch 2, cl) in next ch-3 sp, ch 3, sc in next ch-3 sp, ch 3] 14 [15, 16, 17] times, (cl, ch 2) twice and cl

in next ch-3 sp, ch 3, [sc in next ch-3 sp, ch 3, (cl, ch 2, cl) in next ch-3 sp, ch 3] around, join in first sc, turn.

Rnd 24: Sl st in each st to next ch-2 sp, ch 1, (sc, ch 3, sc) in same sp, [(2 tr, ch 3, 2 tr) in next sc, (sc, ch 3, sc) in next ch-2 sp] 1 [2, 3, 4] time(s), sc in next cl, (sc, ch 3, sc) in next ch-2 sp, [(2 tr, ch 3, 2 tr) in next sc, (sc, ch 3, sc) in next ch-2 sp] 14 [15, 16, 17] times, sc in next cl, (sc, ch 3, sc) in next ch-2 sp, (2 tr, ch 3, 2 tr) in next sc, [(sc, ch 3, sc) in next ch-2 sp, (2 tr, ch 3, 2 tr) in next sc] around, join in first sc, turn.

Rnd 25: Sl st in each st to next ch-3 sp, ch 1, sc in same sp, ch 3, [(cl, ch 2, cl) in next ch-3 sp, ch 3, sc in next ch-3 sp, ch 3] 1 [2, 3, 4] time(s), (cl, ch 2, cl) in next ch-3 sp, ch 3, sk next sc, sc in next sc, ch 3, [(cl, ch 2, cl) in next ch-3 sp, ch 3, sc in next ch-3 sp, ch 3] 14 [15, 16, 17] times, (cl, ch 2, cl) in next ch-3 sp, ch 3, sk next sc, sc in next sc, ch 3, (cl, ch 2, cl) in next ch-3 sp, ch 3, [sc in next ch-3 sp, ch 3, (cl, ch 2, cl) in next ch-3 sp, ch 3] around, join in first sc, turn.

Rnds 26–39: [Rep rnds 12 and 13 alternately] 7 times.

BUTTONHOLE BAND & NECK SHAPING
Sizes Small & Medium Only
Row 1: Working in row ends of Fronts, with RS facing, join cotton with sc in last row of Right Front, [2 sc in next row, sc in next row] to neck, ch 2,

CONTINUED ON PAGE 31

Club Chic Dress

BY **PAULA BENNETT**

SKILL LEVEL ◼◼◼◻
INTERMEDIATE

FINISHED SIZES
Instructions given fit woman's 30–34-inch bust (small); changes for 34–38-inch bust (medium), 38–42-inch bust (large) and 42–46-inch bust (X-large) are in [ ].

FINISHED GARMENT MEASUREMENTS
Bust: 34 inches (small) [38 inches (medium), 42 inches (large), 46 inches (X-large)]

MATERIALS
- Gatsby by Katia Yarns fine (sport) weight yarn: 15 [17, 19, 21] oz #16 burgundy/gold metallic
- Size C/2/2.75mm crochet hook or size needed to obtain gauge
- Tapestry needle
- 4 flat ⅜-inch burgundy buttons

GAUGE
15 dc and 6 ch sps in pattern = 4 inches; 6 rows in pattern = 4 inches

PATTERN NOTES
Weave in loose ends as work progresses.

Join rounds with slip stitch unless otherwise stated.

SPECIAL STITCH
Cluster (cl): Yo, insert hook in next st, yo, draw lp through, yo, draw through 2 lps on hook, yo, insert hook in same st, yo, draw lp through, yo, draw through 2 lps on hook, yo, draw through 3 lps on hook.

INSTRUCTIONS

DRESS
Foundation: Dc foundation st (see Foundation Stitch page 172) in 4th ch from hook, [ch 3, dc in top of dc just made] 67 [76, 85, 94] times (piece should measure 30 [34, 38, 42] inches), turn. (68 [77, 86, 96] lps)

Row 1: Sl st in first lp, ch 3 (counts as first dc), dc in same lp, 2 dc in each lp across, turn. (136 [154, 172, 190] dc)

Row 2: Ch 3, dc in each st across, turn.

Row 3: (Ch 2, dc) in first st (counts as first cl), *ch 4, sk next 2 sts, cl (see Special Stitch), rep from * across, turn. (46 cls, 45 ch sps [52 cls, 51 ch sps; 58 cls, 57 ch sps; 64 cls, 63 ch sps])

Row 4 (RS): Ch 3, dc in first cl, 4 dc in next ch sp, ch 3, sc in next ch sp, ch 3, [6 dc in next ch sp, ch 3, sc in next ch sp, ch 3] across to last ch sp, 4 dc in last ch sp, 2 dc in last cl, turn. (23 [26, 29, 32] dc groups)

Row 5: Ch 3, dc in next dc, ch 5, sk each dc throughout unless otherwise stated, [dc in next ch-3 sp, ch 4, dc in next ch-3 sp, ch 5] across to last 2 sts, dc in each of last 2 sts, turn. (48 [54, 60, 66] dc)

Row 6: Ch 3, dc in next dc, 4 dc in first ch-5 sp, ch 3, sc in next ch-4 sp, ch 3, [6 dc in next ch-5 sp, ch 3, sc in next ch-3 sp, ch 3] across to last ch-5 sp, 4 dc in last ch sp, dc in each of last 2 sts, turn.

Rows 7–12: [Rep rows 5 and 6 alternately] 3 times.

Rnd 13: Now working in rnds, ch 3, dc in next dc, ch 5, [dc in next ch-3 sp, ch 4, dc in next ch-3 sp, ch 5] across to last 6 sts, sk next 4 sts, dc in each of last 2 sts, **join** (see Pattern Notes) in 3rd ch of ch-3, turn.

Rnd 14: Sl st in each of next 2 sts, (sl st, ch 3, 5 dc) in first ch-5 sp, [ch 3, sc in next ch-4 sp, ch 3, 6 dc in next ch-5 sp] around, ch 3, sk next st, sc in next st, ch 3, join in 3rd ch of ch-3, turn.

Rnd 15: Sl st in first ch-3 sp, ch

8 (counts as first dc, ch-5), dc in next ch-3 sp, ch 5, [dc in next ch-3 sp, ch 5] around, join in 3rd ch of ch-8, turn.

Rnd 16: (Sl st, ch 3, 5 dc) in first ch sp, ch 3, sc in next ch sp, ch 3, [6 dc in next ch sp, ch 3, sc in next ch sp, ch 3] around, join in 3rd ch of ch-3, turn.

Rnds 17–33: [Rep rnds 15 and 16 alternately] 9 times, ending with rnd 15.

Rnd 34: (Sl st, ch 3, 6 dc) in first ch sp, ch 3, sc in next ch sp, ch 3, [7 dc in next ch sp, ch 3, sc in next ch sp, ch 3] around, join in 3rd ch of ch-3, turn.

Rnd 35: Sl st in first ch-3 sp, ch 9 (counts as first dc, ch-6), dc in next ch-3 sp, [dc in next ch-3 sp, ch 6] around, join in 3rd ch of ch-9, turn.

Next rnds: Rep rnds 34 and 35 alternately until piece measures 28 inches or desired length, ending with rnd 34. At end of last rnd, fasten off.

TOP EDGING

Row 1: Working on opposite side of foundation ch, with RS of work facing, join with sl st in first lp, ch 3, 2 dc in same lp, 3 dc in each lp across, turn.

Row 2: Ch 1, sc in first st, ch 3, sk next 2 dc, sc in next sp between dc, [ch 3, sk next 3 dc, sc in next sp between dc] across to last 3 dc, ch 3, sk next 2 dc, sc in last dc, turn. (68 [77, 86, 95] ch sps)

Rnd 3: Now working in rnds, working around entire top edge and back openings as follows:

A. Ch 1, sc in first st, 3 sc in each of next 8 [10, 11, 13] ch sps across back;

B. For **first strap**, sc in next ch sp, ch to measures 12½ inches or desired strap length, sk next 16 [17, 18, 19] ch sps, sc in next ch sp (strap made);

C. 3 sc in each of next 16 [19, 24, 27] ch sps across front;

D. Rep step B for **2nd strap**;

E. 3 sc in each of last 8 [10, 11, 13] ch sps across back, sc in last st;

F. Working on RS of back opening in ends of rows, evenly sp sc across;

G. Working in opposite ends of rows on left side of back opening, 3 sc in next row;

H. For **buttonhole**, (sc, ch 5, sc) in next row, 3 sc in each of next 3 rows;

I. Rep step H twice more;

J. (Sc, ch 5, sc) in last row, sc in same st as first sc, join with sl st in first sc, fasten off.

Sew buttons on right back opposite buttonholes. ●

Midnight Scarf

BY **RAYNELDA CALDERON**

SKILL LEVEL ◼◼◼◻
INTERMEDIATE

FINISHED SIZE
4¼ x 43 inches,
including Fringe

MATERIALS
- Bernat Baby super fine (fingering) weight yarn SUPER FINE (1¾ oz/286 yds/50g per ball): 3 balls #00402 white
- Size D/3/3.25mm crochet hook or size needed to obtain gauge
- Tapestry needle

GAUGE
33 hdc foundation sts = 4 inches

PATTERN NOTES
Weave in loose ends as work progresses.

Join rounds with slip stitch unless otherwise stated.

INSTRUCTIONS

SCARF
Foundation row: Work **hdc foundation st** (*see Foundation Stitches on page 172*) 33 times, turn. (*33 hdc*)

Row 1: Ch 1, sc in first hdc, [ch 3, sk next hdc, sc in next hdc] twice, [ch 5, sk next 3 hdc, sc in next hdc] twice, [ch 3, sk next hdc, sc in next hdc] 4 times, [ch 5, sk next 3 hdc, sc in next hdc] twice, [ch 3, sk next hdc, sc in next hdc] twice, turn.

Row 2: Ch 4 (*counts as first dc, ch 1*), sk next sc, sc in next ch-3 sp, ch 3, sc in next ch-3 sp, ch 5, sk next ch-5 sp, dc in next sc, ch 5, sk next ch-5 sp, sc in next ch-3 sp, [ch 3, sc in next ch-3 sp] 3 times, ch 5, sk next ch-5 sp, dc in next sc, ch 5, sk next ch-5 sp, sc in next ch-3 sp, ch 3, sc in next ch-3 sp, ch 1, dc in last sc, turn.

Row 3: Ch 1, sc in next dc, ch 3, sc in next ch-3 sp, ch 5, sk next ch-5 sp, (dc, ch 1, dc) in next dc, ch 5, sk next ch-5 sp, sc in next ch-3 sp, [ch 3, sc in next ch-3 sp] twice, ch 5, sk next ch-5 sp, (dc, ch 1, dc) in next dc, ch 5, sk next ch-5 sp, sc in next ch-3 sp, ch 3, sc in 3rd ch of beg ch-4, turn.

Row 4: Ch 4, sc in next ch-3 sp, ch 5, dc in next ch-1 sp, (ch 1, dc) 4 times in same ch-1 sp, ch 5, sc in next ch-3 sp, ch 3, sc in next ch-3 sp, ch 5, dc in next ch-1 sp, (ch 1, dc) 4 times in same ch-1 sp, ch 5, sc in next ch-3 sp, ch 1, dc in last sc, turn.

Row 5: Ch 8 (*counts as first dc, ch-5*), sk next sc, sk next ch-5 sp, sc in next dc, [ch 3, sc in next dc] 4 times, ch 5, sk next ch-5 sp, dc in next ch-3 sp, ch 5, sk next ch-5 sp, sc in next dc, [ch 3, sc in next dc] 4 times, ch 5, sk next ch-5 sp, dc in next ch, turn.

Row 6: Ch 8, sk next ch-5 sp, sc in next ch-3 sp, [ch 3, sc in next ch-3 sp] 3 times, ch 5, sk next ch-5 sp, dc in next dc, ch 5, sk next ch-5 sp, sc in next ch-3 sp, [ch 3, sc in next ch-3 sp] 3 times, ch 5, sk next 5 chs, dc in next ch, turn.

Row 7: Ch 3 (*counts as first dc*), dc in same st as beg ch-3, ch 5, sk next ch-5 sp, sc in next ch-3 sp, [ch 3, sc in next ch-3 sp] twice, ch 5, (dc, ch 1, dc) in next dc, ch 5, sk next ch-5 sp, sc in next ch-3 sp, [ch 3, sc in next ch-3 sp] twice, ch 5, sk next 5 chs, 2 dc in next ch, turn.

Row 8: Ch 4 (dc, ch 1, dc) in same dc, ch 5, sk next ch-5 sp, sc in next ch-3 sp, ch 3, sc in next ch-3 sp, ch 5, sk next ch-5 sp, dc in next ch-1 sp, (ch 1, dc) 4 times in same ch-1 sp, ch 5, sk next ch-5 sp, sc in next ch-3 sp, ch 3, sc in next ch-3 sp, ch 5, sk next ch-5 sp, sk next dc, dc in next dc, (ch 1, dc) twice in same dc, turn.

Row 9: Ch 1, sc in first dc, [ch

3, sc in next dc] twice, ch 5, sk next ch-5 sp, dc in next ch-3 sp, ch 5, sk next ch-5 sp, sc in next

dc, [ch 3, sc in next dc] 4 times, ch 5, sk next ch-5 sp, dc in next ch-3 sp, ch 5, sk next ch-5 sp,

[sc in next dc, ch 3] twice, sk next ch, sc in next ch, turn.

Row 10: Ch 4, sc in next ch-3 sp, ch 3, sc in next ch-3 sp, ch 5, sk next ch-5 sp, dc in next dc, ch 5, sk next ch-5 sp, sc in next ch-3 sp, [ch 3, sc in next ch-3 sp] 3 times, ch 5, sk next ch-5 sp, dc in next dc, ch 5, sk next ch-5 sp, sc in next ch-3 sp, ch 3, sc in next ch-3 sp, ch 1, dc in last sc, turn.

Row 11: Ch 1, sc in next dc, ch 3, sc in next ch-3 sp, ch 5, sk next ch-5 sp, (dc, ch 1, dc) in next dc, ch 5, sk next ch-5 sp, sc in next ch-3 sp, [ch 3, sc in next ch-3 sp] twice, ch 5, sk next ch-5 sp, (dc, ch 1, dc) in next dc, ch 5, sk next ch-5 sp, sc in next ch-3 sp, ch 3, sk next sc, sc in 3rd ch of beg ch-4, turn.

[Rep rows 4–11 consecutively] 15 times or to desired length.

TRIM
Rnd 1: Work 33 hdc evenly sp across last row of Scarf, ch 1 to turn corner, sc evenly sp down side edge of rows to bottom edge, working across 33 st edge, ch 1, hdc in same st as last st, ch 20, 3 sc in 3rd ch from hook, ch 17, sl st in same st as last hdc, *sl st in each of next 2 hdc, ch 20, 3 sc in 3rd ch from hook, ch 17, sl st in same hdc of last sl st*, rep from * to * across to corner, sc evenly sp across side edge of row to top edge of first 33 hdc sts worked, ch 20, 3 sc in 3rd ch from hook, ch 17, sl st in same st as last hdc, rep from * to * across edge, join in ch-1 sp at corner, fasten off. ●

Ahoy Mate

BY **PAM NOEL**

SKILL LEVEL ▰▰▰▰
EXPERIENCED

FINISHED SIZES
Instructions given fit men's small *(36-inch chest)*; changes for medium *(40-inch chest)* and large *(44-inch chest)* are in [ ].

FINISHED GARMENT MEASUREMENTS
Chest: 40½ inches *(small)*; [44½ inches *(medium)*, 48 inches *(large)*]

Length: 24½ inches *(small)*; [24½ inches *(medium)*, 26½ inches *(large)*]

MATERIALS
- Red Heart Sport light (light worsted) weight yarn (2½ oz/165 yds/70g per skein):
  8 [8, 9] skeins #853 soft navy
  6 [8, 8] skeins #1 white
- Size H/8/5mm crochet hook or size needed to obtain gauge
- Yarn needle
- Stitch markers

GAUGE
16 sts = 4 inches; 11 rows = 4 inches

PATTERN NOTES
Weave in loose ends as work progresses.

Join rounds with slip stitch unless otherwise stated.

SPECIAL STITCH
Cable stitch (cable st): (Yo, insert hook around indicated dc on front of work from right to left, yo, draw up a 1-inch lp) 3 times, yo, draw through all lps on hook, ch 1 to lock.

INSTRUCTIONS

BACK
Row 1: Starting at bottom edge, with white, work **dc foundation st** *(see Foundation Stitches on page 172)* 81 [89, 97] times, turn. *(81 [89, 97] dc)*

Row 2: Ch 1, sc in each st across, turn.

Row 3: Ch 3 *(counts as first dc)*, *fptr *(see Stitch Guide)* around next dc in row below next sc, dc in next st, rep from * 39 [43-47] times, turn. *(81 [89, 97] sts)*

Row 4: Rep row 2.

Row 5: Ch 3, *dc in next st, fptr around next dc in row below next sc, rep from * 38 [42, 46] times, dc in each of last 2 sts, turn.

Rep rows 2–5 for pattern, working 8 more rows with white, then alternate soft navy and white every 12 rows until Back measures 22 [22, 24] inches, then fasten off.

FRONT
Rows 1 & 2: Rep Rows 1 and 2 of Back.

Row 3: Ch 3, *fptr around next dc in row below next sc, dc in next st*, rep from * to * 6 [8, 10] times, sc in next st, **sk next st, **cable st** *(see Special Stitch)* around next dc directly below next sc, dc in sc directly above cable st just worked and in next sc, work cable st directly below last dc worked, sk 1 sc, dc in next st**, rep from * to * 5 times, rep from ** to ** once, rep from * to * 5 times, rep from ** to ** once, rep from * to * 5 times, rep from ** to ** once, dc in next st, rep from * to * 7 [9, 11] times, turn.

Row 4: Rep row 2 of Back.

Row 5: Ch 3, dc in next st, *fptr around next dc in row below next sc, dc in next st*, rep from * to * 6 [8, 10] times, **sk next st, work cable st around next dc directly below next sc, dc in sc directly above cable st just worked and in next st, work cable st around next dc directly below last dc worked, sk 1 sc,

dc in next st**, dc in next st, rep from * to * 4 times, dc in next st, rep from ** to ** once, dc in next st, rep from * to * 4 times, dc in next st, rep from ** to ** once, dc in next st, rep from * to * 4 times, dc in next st, rep from ** to ** once, rep from * to * 7 [9, 11] times, dc in last st, turn.

Rows 6–70 [6–70, 6–72]: Rep rows 2–5 for pattern, working 8 more rows with white, then alternate soft navy and white every 12 rows as for Back.

First Neck & Shoulder Shaping
Note: Continue working in established st and color pattern.

Place st markers around center 19 [19, 21] sts for neck opening.

Row 71 [71, 73]: Work in pattern across next 31 [35, 38] sts, turn.

Row 72 [72, 74]: Ch 1, sl st in each of 1 [1, 2] sts, ch 1, **sc dec** *(see Stitch Guide)* in next 2 sts, sc in each rem st across, turn.

Row 73 [73, 75]: Work in established pattern across, turn.

Row 74 [74, 76]: Ch 1, sc dec in next 2 sts, sc in each rem st across, turn.

Small & Medium Sizes Only
Rows 75–82: [Rep rows 73 and 74 alternately] 4 times. At the end of last rep, fasten off.

Large Size Only
Rows 77–84: [Rep rows 75 and 76 alternately] 4 times. At the end of last rep, fasten off.

2nd Neck & Shoulder Shaping
Row 71 [71, 73]: Sk center 19 [19, 21] sts previously marked, join yarn in next st, ch 3, work in established pattern across rem sts, turn.

Row 72 [72, 74]: Ch 1, sc in each st across to last 2 [2, 3] sts, sk last 2 [2, 3] sts, turn.

Row 73 [73, 75]: Work in established pattern across, turn.

Row 74 [74, 76]: Ch 1, sc in each st across to last 2 sts, sc dec in next 2 sts, turn.

Rows 75–82 [75–82, 77–84]: Rep rows 73 and 74 [73 and 74, 75 and 76]. At the end of last rep, fasten off.

SLEEVE
Make 2.
Note: Use same color sequence as Back and Front.

Row 1: Beg at wrist of Sleeve, with white, work dc foundation ch 39 [41, 43] times, turn. *(39 [41, 43] dc)*

Row 2: Ch 1, sc in each st across, turn.

Row 3: Ch 3, dc in same st as ch-3, *fptr around next dc in row below next sc, dc in next sc, rep from * across, 2 dc in last st, turn.

Rows 4–23 [4–25, 4–27]: [Rep rows 2 and 3 alternately] 10 [11, 12] times.

Row 24 [26, 28]: Rep row 2.

Row 25 [27, 29]: Ch 3, *fptr around next dc in row below next sc, dc in next st, rep from * across, turn.

Row 26 [28, 30]: Rep row 2.

Row 27 [29, 31]: Ch 3, dc in next st, *fptr around next dc in row below next sc, dc in next st, rep from * across, dc in last st, turn.

Rep rows 24–27 [26–29, 28–31] until Sleeve measures 15½ [16, 16½] inches, fasten off.

JOINING
With RS tog, sew Front and Back shoulder seams. Center Sleeve over shoulder seam on each side and sew to body. Sew side and Sleeve seams.

NECKLINE RIBBING
Rnd 1: With RS facing, attach soft navy at center back neckline with sl st, ch 3 *(counts as first dc)*, work 77 [77, 79] dc evenly sp around, join in 3rd ch of ch-3, **do not turn**. *(78 [78, 79] dc)*

Rnd 2: Ch 3, [**fpdc** *(see Stitch Guide)* around next dc, **bpdc** *(see Stitch Guide)* around next dc] around, join in 3rd ch of ch-3, do not turn.

Rnds 3–6: Ch 3, [fpdc around fpdc, bpdc around bpdc] around, join in 3rd ch of ch-3. At the end of rnd 6, fasten off.

SLEEVE RIBBING
Make 2.
Rnd 1: With RS facing, attach soft navy with sl st at Sleeve seam, ch 3, work 33 [35, 37] dc evenly sp around, join in 3rd ch of ch-3, **do not turn**. *(34 [36, 38] dc)*

Rnd 2: Ch 3, [fpdc around next dc, bpdc around next dc] around, join in 3rd ch of beg ch-3, do not turn.

Rnds 3–8: Rep rnd 3 of Neckline Ribbing.

At the end of rnd 8, fasten off.

BOTTOM RIBBING
Rnd 1: With RS facing, attach soft navy with sl st at side seam, ch 3, work 163 [167, 171] dc evenly sp around bottom edge of Sweater, join in 3rd ch of beg ch-3, **do not turn**. *(164 [168, 172] dc)*

Rnds 2–11: Rep rnds 2–11 of Sleeve Ribbing. At the end of last rep, fasten off. ●

Braided Scarf

BY BELINDA CARTER

SKILL LEVEL
INTERMEDIATE

FINISHED SIZE
64 inches long, including Tassels

MATERIALS
- Moda Dea Tweedle Dee bulky (chunky) weight yarn (3½ oz/155 yds/100g per skein): 1 skein #8961 cherry cola
- Size L/11/8mm crochet hook or size needed to obtain gauge
- Tapestry needle
- 4-inch square cardboard

GAUGE
11 sts = 5 inches

PATTERN NOTE
Weave in loose ends as work progresses.

INSTRUCTIONS

BRAID STRIP
Make 3.
Row 1: Leaving a 10-inch length at beg, work **sc foundation st** *(see Foundation Stitches on page 172)* 175 times *(to measure approximately 80 inches)*, leaving 10-inch length, fasten off. *(175 sc)*

BRAIDING
Holding top of the 3 Braid Strips tog, tie beg 10-inch ends in knot over first couple of sts. Loosely braid tog until 56 inches from beg, pull ending tails to unravel excess sts, leaving a 10-inch length, fasten off. Tie ending lengths tog over last couple of sts.

BAND
Make 2.
[Work sc foundation ch] 6 times, leaving a length of yarn, fasten off.

Sew first and last st tog to create ring, slide ring onto end of Scarf.

TASSEL
Make 2.
Wrap yarn around cardboard 30 times, fasten off. Cut end so that there are 30 strands of yarn 8 inches long. Using the scarf 10-inch lengths, securely tie the 30 Tassel strands tog in the middle. Pull Band down over tassel strands so that it's positioned 1 inch from top of Tassel. Trim Tassel ends as desired. ●

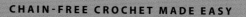

Lacy Lavender Coat

BY **BELINDA CARTER**

SKILL LEVEL ■■■□ INTERMEDIATE

FINISHED SIZES
Instructions given fit 32–34-inch bust (small); changes for 36–38-inch bust (medium), 40–42-inch bust (large) and 44–46-inch bust (X-large) are in [ ].

FINISHED GARMENT MEASUREMENTS
Bust: 40 inches (small), [44 inches (medium), 48 inches (large) and 52 inches (X-large)]

MATERIALS
- Brown Sheep Company Cotton Fleece medium (worsted) weight yarn (3½ oz/215 yds per skein): 8 [9, 10, 10] skeins #CW800 prairie lupine
- Size H/8/5mm crochet hook or size needed to obtain gauge
- Tapestry needle
- 4 La Mode® hand painted 1-inch buttons #1202

GAUGE
24 sts = 6 inches; 20 rows = 6 inches

PATTERN NOTES
Weave in loose ends as work progresses.

Join rounds with slip stitch unless otherwise stated.

Make a 6-inch sample swatch to establish gauge. When working actual coat, gauge will change due to weight of Coat.

When working increase and decrease rows, always begin and end row with single crochet stitch. Work increases and decreases on wrong side rows only.

INSTRUCTIONS

BACK
Row 1 (WS): Work **sc foundation st** (see Foundation Stitch page 172), [ch 3, yo 3 times, insert hook in base ch of last st (2 lps below hook), yo, draw through, {yo, draw through 2 lps on hook} 3 times (3 foundation chs), yo, draw through 1 lp on hook (creates base ch), yo, draw through 2 lps on hook (sc st)] 26 [28, 30, 32] times, turn. (105 [113, 121, 129] sts)

Row 2 (RS): Ch 1, sc, *work 3 foundation ch group below for next 3 sts, ch 1, sk first foundation ch, with hook in front of ch-3 lp, dc in next foundation ch, ch 1, sk last foundation ch, sc in next sc, rep from * across, turn.

Row 3: Ch 1, sc, ch 1, sk ch-1 sp, sc in next dc, *ch 3, sk next 3 sts (ch 1, sc, ch 1), sc in next dc, rep from * across to last 2 sts, ch 1, sk ch-1 sp, sc in last st, turn.

Row 4 (RS): Ch 1, sc, ch 1, sk ch-1 sp, sc in next sc, *ch 1, with hook in front of ch-3 sp, dc in sk sc 2 rows below, ch 1, sc in next sc, rep from * across to last 2 sts, ch 1, sk ch-1 sp, sc in last st, turn.

Row 5 (WS): Ch 1, sc, *ch 3, sk next 3 sts (ch 1, sc, ch 1)**, sc in next dc, rep from * across, ending last rep at **, sc in last st, turn.

Row 6 (RS): Ch 1, sc, *ch 1, with hook in front of ch-3 sp, dc in sk sc 2 rows below, ch 1, sc in next sc, rep from * across, turn.

Rep rows 3–6 for pattern until 18 rows from beg.

Continue working in established pattern, at the same time, keeping with established pattern as much as possible, *[**dec** (see Stitch Guide) in 2 sts at each end of next row, work 3 rows with no dec] 3 times, dec at each end of next row, work 5 rows with no dec, rep from * twice, end of last rep 81 [89, 97, 105] sts rem.

Continue working in established pattern for 2 rows.

Armhole Shaping

Continue working in established pattern, at the same time, keeping in pattern as much as possible, dec 6 [6, 8, 8] sts on each end of next row. *(69 [77, 81, 89] sts)*

Continue working in established pattern, at the same time, keeping with pattern as much as possible, [work 1 row with no dec, dec 2 sts at each end of next row] 3 [4, 4, 5] times, last row will have 57 [61, 65, 69] sts.

Continue working in established pattern for 13 [13, 15, 13] rows.

First Neck Shaping

Row 1: Work established pattern across 17 [19, 19, 21] sts, turn.

Row 2: Work established pattern across, fasten off.

2nd Neck Shaping

Sk next 23 [23, 27, 27] sts, attach yarn in next st, rep First Neck Shaping.

FRONT
Make 2.

Row 1 (WS): Ch 2, insert hook in 2nd ch from hook, yo, draw up a lp, yo, draw through 1 lp on hook, yo, draw through 2 lps on hook, [ch 3, yo 3 times, insert hook in base ch of last st, yo, draw through, {yo, draw through 2 lps on hook} 3 times, yo, draw through 1 lp on hook, yo, draw through 2 lps on hook]

13 [14, 15, 16] times, turn. *(53 [57, 61, 65] sts)*

Row 2 (RS): Ch 1, sc, *work 3 foundation ch group below for next 3 sts, ch 1, sk first foundation ch, with hook in front of ch-3 lp, dc in next foundation ch, ch 1, sk last foundation ch, sc in next sc, rep from * across, turn.

Work rows 3–6 of Back for pattern until 18 rows from beg.

Continue in established pattern, at the same time, keeping with established pattern as much as possible, *[dec 1 st at arm edge on next row, work 3 rows with no dec] 3 times, dec 1 st at arm edge on next row, work 5 rows with no dec] rep from * once, then [dec 1 st at arm edge on next row, work 3 rows with no dec] twice, dec 1 st at arm edge on next row, last row will have 42 [46, 50, 54] sts.

On rem Front rows, continue working in established pattern except on row 4 and on row 6 place hook in back of ch-3 sp to work dc in sk sc 2 rows below instead of placing hook in front of ch-3 sp.

Continue working in established pattern, at the same time, keeping with established pattern as much as possible, work 3 rows with no dec, dec 1 st at arm edge on next row, work 7 rows with no dec, last row will have 41 [45, 49, 53] sts.

Armhole Shaping
Continue working in

established pattern, at the same time, keeping with established pattern as much as possible, dec 6 [6, 8, 8] sts at arm edge on next row. *(35 [39, 41, 45] sts)*

Continue working in established pattern, at the same time, keeping with established pattern as much as possible, [work 1 row with no dec, dec 2 sts at arm edge on next row] 3 [4, 4, 5] times. *(29 [31, 33, 35] sts)*

COLLAR
With WS facing, attach yarn to front as follows: On right front, attach yarn in 13th st from neck opening. On left front, attach yarn in first st at neck opening.

Ch 1, work established pattern across 13 sts, turn.

Continue working in established pattern for 17 [17, 19, 19] more rows. At the end of last rep, fasten off.

SLEEVE
Make 2.
Row 1 (WS): Ch 2, insert hook in 2nd ch from hook, yo, draw through, yo, draw through 1 lp on hook, yo, draw through 2 lps on hook, [ch 3, yo 3 times, insert hook in base ch of last st, yo, draw through, {yo, draw through 2 lps on hook} 3 times, yo, draw through 1 lp on hook, yo, draw through 2 lps on hook] 8 [8, 10, 10] times, turn. *(33 [33, 41, 41] sts)*

Row 2 (RS): Ch 1, sc, *work in 3 foundation ch group below for next 3 sts, ch 1, sk first foundation ch, with hook in front of ch-3

sp, dc in next foundation ch, ch 1, sk last foundation ch, sc in next sc, rep from * across, turn.

Work rows 3–6 of Back for pattern, at the same time, keeping with established pattern as much as possible, inc 1 st at each end of next row, then inc 1 st at each end of every 2nd row 2 [6, 2, 6] times, then inc 1 st each end of every 4th row 9 [7, 9, 7] times. *(57 [61, 65, 69] sts)*

Continue working in established pattern for 5 [5, 7, 7] rows.

Cap Shaping
Continue working in established pattern, at the same time keeping with established pattern as much as possible, dec 6 [6, 8, 8] sts on each end of next row. *(45 [49, 49, 53] sts)*

Keeping with established pattern as much as possible, [work 1 row with no dec, dec 2 sts at each end of next row] 3 [3, 2, 2] times. *(33 [37, 41, 45] sts)*

Work in established pattern for 1 [1, 3, 3] rows with no dec.

Keeping with established pattern as much as possible, [dec 4 sts at each end of next row, work 1 row with no dec] twice, fasten off. *(17 [21, 25, 29] sts)*

ASSEMBLY
Sew shoulder seams, Sleeves into arm openings and side and Sleeve seams. Sew last row of left front Collar to last row of right front Collar, then sew

Collar to back neck opening easing in fullness.

BOTTOM LACE

Row 1: With RS facing, working in unused lps of foundation, attach yarn with sl st at opening, ch 1, sc in same lp as beg sl st, *ch 2, sk next 3 foundation ch, work [dc, ch 1] 5 times in base ch *(where sc st was worked)*, sk next 3 foundation ch, sc in next base ch *(where sc was worked)*, rep from * across, turn.

Row 2: Ch 1, sc, ch 3, sk ch-1 sp, sc in next ch-1 sp, *[ch 3, sc in next ch-1 sp] 3 times**, ch 2, sk next 2 ch-1 sps, sc in next ch-1 sp, rep from * across to last ch-1 sp, ending last rep at **, ch 3, sk next ch-1 sp, sc in last st, fasten off.

SLEEVE LACE

Rnd 1: With RS facing, working in unused lps of foundation, attach yarn with sl st at seam, ch 1, sc in same lp as beg sl st, *ch 1, sk next 3 foundation ch, work [dc, ch 1] 5 times in base ch *(where sc was worked)*, sk next 3 foundation ch**, sc in next base ch *(where sc was worked)*, rep from * around, ending last rep at **, join in beg sc st, turn.

Rnd 2: Sl st in ch-1 sp, sl st in dc, sl st in next ch-1 sp, ch 1, sc in same sp as last sl st, *[ch 3, sc in next ch-1 sp] 3 times, ch 2, sk next 2 ch-1 sps**, sc in next ch-1 sp, rep from * around, ending last rep at **, join in beg sc, fasten off.

FRONT & COLLAR EDGING

Row 1: With RS facing, attach yarn at right front opening with sl st in ch-3 lp, ch 1, sc in end of first row on front, *ch 1, sk end of next row, sc in end of next row, rep from * up right Front around Collar and down left Front, ch 1, sc in ch-3 lp, turn.

Row 2: [Ch 3, sk ch-1 sp, sl st in next sc] across, fasten off.

BUTTONS

Coat will be fastened using ch-3 sps on edging for buttonholes. Using lps for placement guide, sew first button to left Front where pattern changes from crocheting with hook in front of ch-3 sp to crocheting with hook in back of ch-3 sp, then sew 3 more buttons going down left Front, spacing buttons 2 inches apart.

FINISHING

Fold Collar back, beg fold where first button is sewn. ●

Shoulder Wrap

BY **LENA CHAMBERLAIN**

SKILL LEVEL

INTERMEDIATE

FINISHED SIZE
60¼ inches across

MATERIALS
- Bernat Baby super fine (fingering) weight yarn (1¾ oz/286 yds/50g per ball): 3 balls #402 white
- Size G/6/4mm crochet hook or size needed to obtain gauge
- Tapestry needle

GAUGE
6 sc = 1 inch; 12 sc rows = 2 inches; 3 love knots = 3 inches; 4 love knot rows = 2 inches

PATTERN NOTES
Weave in loose ends as work progresses.

Join rounds with slip stitch unless otherwise stated.

SPECIAL STITCHES
Double love knot: Draw up long lp to measure ½ inch, yo, draw through lp, sc in back strand of long lp, draw up long lp to measure ½ inch, yo draw through lp, sc in back strand of long lp.

Love knot: Draw up long lp on hook to measure ½ inch, yo, draw through lp, sc in back strand of long lp.

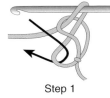

Step 1

Step 2

Step 3

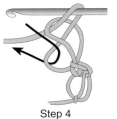

Step 4

Step 5

Double Love Knot

Completed
Double Love Knot

INSTRUCTIONS

CUFF
Make 2.
Row 1: Starting at cuff, work **sc foundation st** *(see Foundation Stitches on page 172)* 6 times, turn. *(6 sc)*

Rows 2–50: Working in **back lps** *(see Stitch Guide)*, ch 1, sc in each st across, turn. *(6 sc)*

Row 51: Matching row 1 to row 50 and working through both thicknesses, sl st in each st across.

Row 52: Working in ends of rows, ch 1, sc in each of next 50 rows, turn. *(50 sc)*

Row 53: Ch 4 *(counts as first dc, ch-1)*, sk next st, [dc in next st, ch 1, sk next st] 23 times, dc in each of next 2 sts, turn. *(26 dc, 24 ch-1 sps)*

Row 54: Ch 1, sc in each dc and in each ch-1 sp across, turn. For **first Cuff**, fasten off, for **2nd**

Cuff, do not fasten off.

SHOULDER & SLEEVE
Row 1: Ch 3, **love knot** (see Special Stitches), sk first st, sc in next st, ***double love knot** (see Special Stitches), sk next st, sc in next st, rep from * 22 times,

love knot, dc in last st, turn. *(23 double love knots, 2 love knots)*

Rows 2–75 or until piece fits loosely across shoulders to other wrist: Ch 3, love knot, sk first love knot, sc in next sc, [double love knot, sc in center of

next double love knot] 23 times, love knot, dc in last st, turn. At end of row 75, fasten off.

Easing to fit, sew double love knots and love knots of row 75 on Shoulder and Sleeve to row 54 of first Cuff. ●

Brimmed Hat

BY **KATHY SEHRER**

SKILL LEVEL ■□□□
BEGINNER

FINISHED SIZE
19½ inches in diameter

MATERIALS
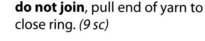
- Medium (worsted) weight yarn:
  3 oz red
  1½ oz black
- Size G/6/4mm crochet hook or size needed to obtain gauge
- Tapestry needle
- Stitch marker

GAUGE
4 sc = 1 inch; 4 sc rnds = 1 inch

PATTERN NOTES
Weave in loose ends as work progresses.

Join rounds with slip stitch unless otherwise stated.

Use stitch marker to mark rounds that are not joined.

Use size F hook for smaller Hat size and size H hook for larger Hat size.

INSTRUCTIONS

CROWN
Rnd 1: With red, make **slip ring** *(see Foundation Stitches on page 172)*, times, ch 1, 9 sc in ring,

do not join, pull end of yarn to close ring. *(9 sc)*

Rnd 2: 2 sc in each sc around. *(18 sc)*

Rnd 3: [Sc in next sc, 2 sc in next sc] around. *(27 sc)*

Rnd 4: [Sc in each of next 2 sc, 2 sc in next sc] around. *(36 sc)*

Rnd 5: [Sc in each of next 3 sc, 2 sc in next sc] around. *(45 sc)*

Rnd 6: Sc in each sc around.

Rnd 7: [Sc in each of next 4 sc, 2 sc in next sc] around. *(54 sc)*

Rnd 8: Rep rnd 6.

Rnd 9: [Sc in each of next 5 sc, 2 sc in next sc] around. *(63 sc)*

Rnd 10: Rep rnd 6.

Rnd 11: [Sc in each of next 6 sc, 2 sc in next sc] around. *(72 sc)*

Rnd 12: Rep rnd 6.

Rnd 13: [Sc in each of next 11 sc, 2 sc in next sc] around. *(78 sc)*

Rnds 14–22: Rep rnd 6.

At the end of rnd 22, draw up a lp of black, fasten off red.

Rnds 23–27: With black, sc in each sc around.

At the end of rnd 27, draw up a lp of red, fasten off black.

BRIM
Rnd 28: **Fpsc** *(see Stitch Guide)* in each sc around. *(78 sts)*

Rnd 29: Sc in each st around.

Rnd 30: [Sc in each of next 2 sc, 2 sc in next sc] 26 times. *(104 sc)*

Rnd 31: Rep rnd 29.

Rnd 32: [Sc in each of next 3 sc, 2 sc in next sc] 26 times. *(130 sc)*

Rnd 33: Rep rnd 29.

Rnd 34: [Sc in each of next 4 sc, 2 sc in next sc] 26 times. *(156 sc)*

Rnd 35: Rep rnd 29.

Rnd 36: Sc around, sk 31 sc evenly sp around. *(125 sc)*

Rnd 37: Rep rnd 29.

Rnd 38: Rep rnd 36. *(94 sc)*

Rnd 39: Rep rnd 29, sl st in next st, fasten off. ●

Sweater Jacket

BY **MARGARET HUBERT**

SKILL LEVEL ⬛⬛⬜⬜
INTERMEDIATE

FINISHED SIZES
Instructions given fit 32–34-inch bust *(small)*; changes for 36–38-inch bust *(medium)*, and 40–42-inch bust *(large)* are in [ ].

FINISHED GARMENT MEASUREMENTS
Bust: 36 inches *(small)*, [38 inches *(medium)*, 40 inches *(large)*]

MATERIALS
- Patons SWS medium (worsted) weight yarn (2¾ oz/110 yds/80g per ball): 11 [12, 13] balls #70013 natural earth
- Sizes I/9/5.5mm and K/10½/6.5mm crochet hooks or sizes needed to obtain gauge
- Tapestry needle
- Straight or safety pins
- 1¾-inch buttons: 3

GAUGES
Size I hook: 14 sts = 4 inches;

Size K hook: 12 body sts = 4 inches; 11 sleeve sts = 4 inches

PATTERN NOTES
Weave in loose ends as work progresses.

Waist shaping is achieved by changing hook size.

Rows 2 and 3 of Back establish Sweater Jacket pattern unless otherwise stated.

INSTRUCTIONS

BACK
Foundation row: Starting at bottom edge with size K hook, work **sc foundation st** *(see Foundation Stitches on page 172)* 55 [59, 63] times, turn. *(55 [59, 63] sc)*

Row 1: Ch 2 *(counts as first sc, ch- 1)*, sk first 2 sts, [sc in next st, ch 1, sk 1 st] across, sc in beg ch, turn.

Row 2: Ch 1 *(counts as sc)*, sk first sc, sc in next ch-1 sp, [ch 1, sk next sc, sc in next ch-1 sp] across, 1 sc in beg ch-2, turn.

Row 3: Ch 2, sk first 2 sc, sc in next ch-1 sp, [ch 1, sk next sc, sc in next ch-1 sp] across, sc in beg ch-1, turn.

Rep rows 2 and 3 for 5½ [6, 6½] inches from beg. Working waistline, change to size I hook and continue in established pattern of rows 2 and 3 for 2 [2, 2] inches, change back to size K hook and continue in established pattern of rows 2 and 3 until Back measures 13½ [14, 14½] inches from beg.

Armhole Shaping
Sl st in each of next 2 [2, 2] sts, ch 1, work in established pattern to within 2 [2, 2] sts of opposite edge, turn.

Working established pattern on 51 [55, 59] sts until Armhole measures 7½ [8, 8½] inches, fasten off.

LEFT FRONT
Foundation row: Starting at bottom edge with size K hook, work sc foundation st 31 [33, 35] times.

Row 1: Rep row 1 of Back.

Rep rows 2 and 3 of Back to the same length as Back to Armhole Shaping, ending at arm edge.

Armhole Shaping
Sl st in each of 2 [2, 2] sts, work across row. Continue in established pattern on rem 29 [31, 33] sts until Armhole measures 5 [5½, 6] inches, ending at arm edge.

Neck Shaping
Work in established pattern across 18 [19, 20] sts, leaving rem 11 [12, 13] sts unworked, turn.

5 [5½, 6] inches, ending at front center edge.

Neck Shaping

Sl st in each of next 11 [12, 13] sts, ch 1, continue in established pattern across row, turn. Continue in established pattern on 18 [19, 20] sts, dec 1 st at neck edge every row 4 [4, 4] times. Work in established pattern on 14 [15, 16] sts until Armhole measures 7½ [8, 8½] inches from beg, fasten off.

SLEEVE
Make 2.
Note: Sleeves are crocheted vertically and shaped by working hdc at end of every 4th row.

Foundation row: With size K hook, work sc foundation st 43 [45, 47] times, turn. *(43 [45, 47] sc)*

Row 1: Ch 1 *(counts as first sc)*, sk first st, working in **back lps** *(see Stitch Guide)* sc in each of next 29 sts, hdc in each of next 12 [14, 16], hdc in end ch, turn.

Row 2: Ch 1, sk first st, sc in back lps of each of next 41 [43, 45] sts, sc in beg ch-1, turn.

Rows 3 & 4: Rep row 2.

Rep rows 1–4 for 52 [56, 60] rows, fasten off. *(26, 28, 30 ridges)*

COLLAR
Note: Collar is shaping is done by working hdc at end of every 4th row.

Foundation row: With size K hook, work sc foundation st 15

Working on rem 18 [19, 20] sts, continue in established pattern, **dec 1 st** *(see Stitch Guide)* at neck edge every row 4 [4, 4] times. Work in established pattern on 14 [15, 16] sts until armhole measures 7½ [8, 8½] inches from beg, fasten off.

RIGHT FRONT
Foundation row: Starting at bottom edge with size K hook, work sc foundation ch st 31 [33, 35] times.

Row 1: Rep row 1 of Back.

Rep rows 2 and 3 of Back to the same length as Back to Armhole Shaping, ending at center front edge.

Armhole Shaping
Work across row to last 2 [2, 2] sts, turn.

Ch 1, continue in established pattern on rem 29 [31, 33] sts until armhole measures

[17, 19] times, turn. *(15 [17, 19] sc)*

Row 1: Ch 1, sk first st, working in back lps, sc in each of next 1 [2, 3] sts, hdc in each of next 12 [13, 14] sts, hdc in end ch, turn.

Row 2: Ch 1, sk first st, sc in back lp of each of next 13 [15, 17] sts, sc in end ch, turn.

Rows 3 & 4: Rep row 2.

Rep rows 1–4 for 56 [58, 60] rows, fasten off. *(28 [29, 30] ridges)*

ASSEMBLY
Sew shoulder seams. Fold Sleeve in half, pin center of Sleeve to shoulder seam, sew Sleeve in place. Sew Sleeve and side seams.

RIGHT FRONT BUTTONHOLE EDGE
Note: *Using pins, divide fronts into 4 equal parts making it easier to pick up sts evenly sp.*

Row 1: With RS facing, starting at bottom edge with size I hook, join yarn with sl st, ch 1, work 56 [60, 64] sc, turn. *(14 [15, 16] sts in each section, remove pins)*

Row 2: Ch 1, sk first sc, sc in each of next 54 [58, 62] sc, sc in end ch, turn.

Row 3: Ch 1, sk first sc, sc in each of next 10 [12, 14] sc, [ch 5, sk next 4 sc, sc in each of next 9 sc] twice, ch 5, sk next 44 sc, sc in each of next 14 [16, 18] sc, sc in end ch, turn. *(3 buttonholes)*

Row 4: Ch 1, sk first sc, sc in each of next 14 [16, 18] sc, [4 sc in next ch-5 sp, sc in each of next 9 sc] 3 times, sc in each of last 1 [2, 3] sc, sc in end ch, turn.

Row 5: Rep row 2, fasten off.

LEFT FRONT BUTTON BAND
Row 1: With RS facing, starting at top left front with size I hook, join yarn with sl st, ch 1, work 56 [60, 64] sc, turn. *(14 [15, 16] sts in each section, remove pins)*

Rows 2–5: Ch 1, sk first sc, sc in each of next 54 [58, 62] sc, sc in end ch, turn.

At the end of row 5, fasten off.

FINISHING
Fold Collar in half, with RS of Collar to WS of Jacket, pin center of Collar to center of Back, pin ends of Collar to end of Bands easing in fullness, sew Collar to Jacket.

Sew buttons to Left Front opposite buttonholes. ●

Fashion Tunic CONTINUED FROM PAGE 11

working in bottom of foundation ch, sc in each st around neck, ch 2, working in row ends of Left Front, sc in first row, [2 sc in next row, sc in next row to end, turn. *(189 [197] sc)*

Sizes Large & X-Large Only
Row 1: Working in row ends of Fronts, with RS facing, join cotton with sc in last row of Right Front, sc in same sp, [2 sc in next row, sc in next row] to neck, ch 2, working in bottom of foundation ch, sc in each st around neck, ch 2, working in row ends of Left Front, sc in first row, [2 sc in next row, sc in next row to end, 2 sc in last row, turn. *([212, 220] sc)*

Row 2: Ch 1, [sc in each st up to next ch-2 sp, ch 2, sk next ch-2 sp] twice, sc in each st across, turn.

Row 3: Ch 4, sk next st, [dc in next st, ch 1, sk next st] up to next ch-2 sp, dc in next ch-2 sp, turn, leaving rem sts unworked. *(18 [18, 21, 21] dc)*

Rows 4 & 5: Ch 4, dc in next st, [ch 1, dc in next st] across, turn. At the end of row 5, fasten off.

BUTTON BAND

Row 1: With RS facing, join cotton with sl st in ch-2 sp on Left Front, ch 4, sk next st, dc in next st, [ch 1, sk next st, dc in next st] across, turn. *(18 [18, 21, 21] dc)*

Rows 2 & 3: Ch 4, dc in next st, [ch 1, dc in next st] across, turn. At the end of row 3, fasten off.

COLLAR

Row 1: With RS facing, join cotton with sl st in top of last st of last row on Button Band, ch 4, [dc, ch 1 in next row] twice, dc in next st, [ch 1, sk next st, dc in next st] up to Button Band, dc in next st, [ch 1, dc in next row] twice, turn. *(84 [88, 92, 96] dc)*

Rows 2 & 3: Ch 4, dc in next st, [ch 1, sk ch-1 sp, dc in next st] across, turn. At the end of row 3, fasten off.

EDGING

Row 1: With RS facing, working in row ends of Buttonhole Band, join cotton with sc in first row, sc in next row, 2 sc in next 3 rows, ch 2, sc in top of first st of last row on Buttonhole Band, [sc in next ch-1 sp, sc in next st] up to Collar, 2 sc in next 3 rows of collar, ch 2, sc in first st of last row of collar, [sc in next ch-1 sp, sc in next st] up to row ends of opposite side of Collar, ch 2, 2 sc in each of next 3 rows, sc in next st of Button Band, [sc in next ch-1 sp, sc in next st] to end, turn. *(247 [255, 273, 281] sts)*

Row 2: Ch 1, sc in each st to next ch-2 sp, ch 2, sk next ch-2 sp, sc in each of next 7 sts, [sc dec in next 2 sts, sc in each of next 2 sts] 39 [41, 43, 45] times, sc in each of next 4 sts, ch 2, sk next ch-2 sp, sc in each st to next ch-2 sp, sc in ch-2 sp, turn. *(208 [214, 230, 236] sc)*

Row 3: Ch 1, sc in each st to ch-2 sp, ch 3, sk next ch-2 sp, sc in each of next 9 [12, 15, 18] sts, [sc dec in next 2 sts] 12 times, sc in each of next 8 sts, [sc dec in next 2 sts] 3 times, [sc in each of next 2 sts, sc dec in next 2 sts] 3 times, [sc dec in next 2 sts] 3 times, [sc in each of next 2 sts, sc dec next 2 sts tog] 4 times, [sc dec in next 2 sts] twice, sc in each of next 8 sts, [sc dec in next 2 sts] 12 times, sc in each of next 9 [12, 15, 18] sts, ch 3, sk next ch-2 sp, sc in each st to end, leaving a long length for sewing, fasten off. *(170 [176, 192, 198] sts)*

With tapestry needle, st end of Button Band to rnd 1 on Body. Stitch end of Buttonhole Band to top of Button Band. Evenly sp buttons and st in place on Button Band.

SLEEVE
Make 2.

Row 1: With RS facing, join cotton with sl st in top of last st on row 1 of Left Front, (sc, ch 3, sc) in first sk ch-2 sp of armhole, [(2 tr, ch 3, 2 tr) in next sc, (sc, ch 3, sc) in next ch-3 sp] across, join with sl st in first st of row 1 on Back, sl st in each st to top st directly above in next row on Back, turn. *(4 sc, 4 tr)*

Row 2: (**Beg cl**—*see Special Stitches*, ch 2, cl) in next ch-3 sp, [ch 3, sc in next ch-3 sp, ch 3, (cl, ch 2, cl) in next ch-3 sp] across, join with sl st in last of corresponding row on Left Front, sl st in each st to top of st directly above in next row on Front, turn.

Note: Continue to join beg and ending of each row as established in rows 1 and 2 of Sleeve.

Row 3: (Sc, ch 3, sc) in next ch-2 sp, [(2 tr, ch 3, 2 tr) in next sc, (sc, ch 3, sc) in next ch-2 sp] across, join, turn.

Row 4: (Beg cl, ch 2, cl, ch 2, cl) in next ch-3 sp, ch 3, sc in next ch-3 sp, ch 3, (cl, ch 2) twice and cl in next ch-3 sp, join, turn.

Row 5: (Sc, ch 3, sc) in next ch-2 sp, sc in top of next cl, (sc, ch 3, sc) in next ch-2 sp, (2 tr, ch 3, 2 tr) in next sc, (sc, ch 3, sc) in next ch-2 sp, sc in top of next cl, (sc, ch 3, sc) in next ch-2 sp, join, turn.

Row 6: (Cl, ch 2, cl) in next ch-3 sp, ch 3, sk next sc, sc in next sc, ch 3, (cl, ch 2, cl) in next ch-3 sp, ch 3, sc in next ch-3 sp, ch 3, (cl, ch 2, cl) in next ch-3 sp, ch 3, sk next sc, sc in next sc, ch 3, (cl, ch 2, cl) in next ch-3 sp, join, turn.

Row 7: Rep row 3.

Rows 8 & 9: Rep rows 2 and 3.

Row 10: (Cl, ch 2) twice and cl in next ch-3 sp, ch 3, sc in next ch-3 sp, ch 3, [(cl, ch 2, cl) in next ch-3 sp, ch 3, sc in next ch-3 sp, ch 3] up to last ch-3 sp, (cl, ch 2) twice and cl in last sp, join, turn.

Row 11: (Sc, ch 3, sc) in next ch-2 sp, sc in top of next cl, [(sc, ch 3, sc) in next ch-2 sp, (2 tr, ch 3, 2 tr) in next sc] to last 3 cls, (sc, ch 3, sc) in next ch-2 sp, sc in top of next cl, (sc, ch 3, sc) in next ch-2 sp, join, turn.

Row 12: (Cl, ch 2, cl) in next ch-3 sp, ch 3, sk next sc, sc in next sc, ch 3, [(cl, ch 2, cl) in next ch-3 sp, ch 3, sc in next ch-3 sp, ch 3] up to last 2 ch-3 sps, (cl, ch 2, cl) in next ch-3 sp, ch 3, sk next sc, sc in next sc, ch 3, (cl, ch 2, cl) in next ch-3 sp, join, turn.

Row 13: Rep row 3.

Rows 14 & 15: Rep rows 2 and 3.

Rows 16–19: Rep rows 10–13.

Large & X-Large Sizes Only
Rows 20–23: Rep rows 10–13.

All Sizes
Rnd 1: Now working in rnds, (cl, ch 2, cl) in next ch-3 sp, [ch 3, sc in next ch-3 sp, ch 3, (cl, ch 2, cl) in next ch-3 sp] across,

join with sl st in last st of corresponding row, ch 3, sc in center of underarm, ch 3, join in top of first cl of first of this rnd, turn.

Rnd 2: Sl st in each st to next sc, ch 4, (tr, ch 3, 2 tr) in same sp, (sc, ch 3, sc) in next ch-2 sp [(2 tr, ch 3, 2 tr) in next sc, (sc, ch 3, sc) in next ch-2 sp] around, join, turn.

Rnd 3: Sl st in each st to next ch-3 sp, (beg cl, ch 2, cl) in same sp, ch 3, sc in next ch-3 sp, ch 3, [(cl, ch 2, cl) in next ch-3 sp, ch 3, sc in next ch-3 sp, ch 3] around, join, turn.

Rnd 4: Sl st in each st to next sc, ch 4, (tr, ch 2, 2 tr) in same sp, (sc, ch 2, sc) in next ch-2 sp, [(2 tr, ch 2, 2 tr) in next sc, (sc, ch 2, sc) in next ch-2 sp] around, join, turn.

Rnd 5: Sl st in each st to next ch-2 sp, (beg cl, ch 2, cl) in same sp, ch 2, sc in next ch-2 sp, ch 2, [(cl, ch 2, cl) in next ch-2 sp, ch 2, sc in next ch-2 sp, ch 2] around, join, turn.

Rnds 6–33: [Rep rnds 4 and 5 alternately] 14 times.

Rnd 34: Rep rnd 4.

Rnd 35: Sl st in each st to next ch-2 sp, (beg cl, ch 2, cl) in same sp, ch 1, sc in next ch-2 sp, ch 1, [(cl, ch 2, cl) in next ch-2 sp, ch 1, sc in next ch-2 sp, ch 1] around, join, turn.

Rnd 36: Sl st in each st to next sc, ch 4, (tr, ch 2, 2 tr) in same sp, (sc, ch 1, sc) in next ch-2 sp, [(2 tr, ch 2, 2 tr) in next sc, (sc, ch 1, sc) in next ch-2 sp] around, join, turn.

Rnd 37: Sl st in each st to next ch-1 sp, (beg cl, ch 1, cl) in same sp, ch 1, sc in next ch-2 sp, ch 1, [(cl, ch 1, cl) in next ch-1 sp, ch 1, sc in next ch-2 sp, ch 1] around, join, turn.

Rnd 38: Sl st in each st to next sc, ch 4, (tr, ch 1, 2 tr) in same sp, sk next ch-1 sp, (sc, ch 1, sc) in next ch-1 sp, [(2 tr, ch 1, 2 tr) in next sc, sk next ch-1 sp, (cl, ch 1, cl) in next ch-1 sp] around, join, turn.

Rnds 39 & 40 [39–42, 39–42, 39–44]: [Rep rnds 37 and 38 alternately] 1 [2, 2, 3] time(s). At the end of last rep, fasten off. ●

Gift Giving Made Easy

Chapter Contents

Cabled Dog Set

BY **DONNA JONES**

SKILL LEVEL
■■■□ INTERMEDIATE

FINISHED SIZES
Instructions for size small *(20-inch chest)*; changes for medium *(22-inch chest)* and large *(24-inch chest)* are in [ ].

MATERIALS
- Red Heart Super Saver medium (worsted) weight yarn (7 oz/364 yds/198g per skein):
  1 skein #321 gold
- Size H/8/5mm crochet hook or size needed to obtain gauge
- Tapestry needle
- Sewing needle
- Gold sewing thread
- 4 gold ⅝-inch buttons
- Stitch markers

GAUGE
3 dc = 1 inch; 3 dc rows = 1½ inches

PATTERN NOTES
Weave in loose ends as work progresses.

Join with slip stitch as indicated unless otherwise stated.

SPECIAL STITCHES
Popcorn (pc): 4 dc in next st, remove lp from hook, insert hook in first dc of 4-dc group, pick up dropped lp and draw through st on hook.

Cross cable: Sk next 3 sts, fpdtr around each of next 2 post sts, dc behind last 2 sts into 3rd sk st, fpdtr around first sk st, fpdtr around next sk st.

Double crochet joining (dc joining): Yo, insert hook in next st, yo, draw lp through, insert hook in first st in next section, yo, draw through st and first 2 lps on hook, yo, draw through last 2 lps on hook.

Half double crochet-single crochet decrease (hdc-sc dec): Yo, insert hook in next st, yo, draw up lp, insert hook in next st, yo, draw up lp, yo, draw through all 4 lps on hook.

CABLE PATTERN

Note: Work within rows as instructed, beg in row 3 of Sweater.

Row 3 (RS): Fpdc *(see Stitch Guide)* around next st, dc in each of next 2 sts, **pc** *(see Special Stitches)* in next st, dc in each of next 2 sts, **cross cable** *(see Special Stitches)*, dc in each of next 2 sts, pc in next st, dc in

each of next 2 sts, fpdc around next st.

Row 4 (WS): Bpdc *(see Stitch Guide)* around next st, dc in each of next 5 sts, bpdc around each of next 2 sts, dc in next st, bpdc around next 2 sts, dc in each of next 5 sts, bpdc around next st.

Row 5: Fpdc around next st, dc in next st, [pc in next st, dc in next st] twice, fpdc around each of next 2 sts, dc in next st, fpdc around each of next 2 sts, dc in next st, [pc in next st, dc

in next st] twice, fpdc around next st.

Row 6: Bpdc around next st, dc in each of next 5 sts, bpdc around each of next 2 sts, dc in next st, bpdc around each of next 2 sts, dc in each of next 5 sts, bpdc around next st.

CONTINUED ON PAGE 58

Back Scrubber

BY **SHARI JACOBSON**

SKILL LEVEL
EASY

FINISHED SIZE
30 inches long

MATERIALS
- Tahki Cotton Classic light (light worsted) weight yarn (1¾ oz/108 yds/50g per skein):
  1 skein #3472 peach
- Sizes F/5/3.75mm and I/9/5.5mm crochet hooks or size needed to obtain gauge
- Tapestry needle
- 1¼ yd of 72-inch-wide coarse netting
- 2 plastic 2-inch rings

GAUGE
With size I hook and 1 strand peach and 1 strip netting held tog: 5 sc = 1¾ inches; 5 sc rows = 1½ inches

PATTERN NOTES
Weave in loose ends as work progresses.

Join with slip stitch as indicated unless otherwise stated.

Cut netting into 1½-inch-wide strips.

Use netting strip and peach held together as one unless otherwise stated.

INSTRUCTIONS

SCRUBBER
Row 1: Working loosely, with size I hook, work **sc foundation st** *(see Foundation Stitches on page 172)* 5 times, turn. *(5 sc)*

Row 2: Ch 1, sc in each st across, turn.

Rows 3–9: Rep row 2.

Row 10: Ch 1, sc in first sc, 2 sc in next sc, sc in next sc, 2 sc in next sc, sc in last sc, turn. *(7 sc)*

Rows 11–85: Rep row 2.

Row 86: Ch 1, sc in first sc, **sc dec** *(see Stitch Guide)* in next 2 sc, sc in next sc, sc dec in next 2 sc, sc in last sc, turn. *(5 sc)*

Rows 87–95: Rep row 2. At the end of row 95, fasten off.

Rnd 96: Now working in rnds, with size F hook, join peach only with sc in end of any row, sc in ends of row and in sts, adding sts as needed to lay flat with 3 sc in each corner, join in first sc.

Rnd 97: Ch 1, *sc in each st across to corner, 3 sc in center sc, holding ring next to crochet and working over ring and into sc, 2 sc in each st across to next corner sc, 3 sc in center corner, rep from *, sc in each rem sc, join in first sc. Fasten off. ●

Bath Mitt

BY **DONNA SCOTT**

SKILL LEVEL ◼◼◻◻
EASY

FINISHED SIZE
5 inches across x 7 inches long
including Cuff

MATERIALS
• 2 yds 45-inch-wide nylon
  netting color of choice (cut
  into 1-inch-wide strips)
• Size J/10/6mm crochet
  hook or size needed
  to obtain gauge
• Tapestry needle

GAUGE
3 sts = 1 inch; 2 popcorn rows
and 1 sc row = 1¾ inches

PATTERN NOTES
Weave in loose ends as work
progresses.

Join with slip stitch as indicated
unless otherwise stated.

SPECIAL STITCH
Popcorn (pc): 4 dc in next st,
drop lp from hook, insert hook
in first dc of 4-group group,
pick up dropped lp and draw
through st on hook.

INSTRUCTIONS

MITT
Cuff
Row 1: Work **sc foundation st**
(see Foundation Stitches on page

172) 6 times, turn.
(6 sc)

Row 2: Working in
back lps *(see Stitch
Guide)*, ch 1, sc in each
st across, turn. *(6 sc)*

Rows 3–22: Rep row 2.

Row 23: Hold first row
to last row and working
through both thick-
nesses, sl st in each st
across, forming a ridge,
do not fasten off.

Palm
Rnd 1: Working in
ends of rows, ch 1,
(sc, ch 1) in seam *(sc,
ch 1 counts as first
dc)*, evenly sp 19 dc
around next 22 rows,
join in ch-1. *(20 dc)*

Rnd 2: Ch 1, (sc, ch 1,
dc) in first st, sc in next
st, [2 dc in next st, dc in next st]
around, join in first dc. *(30 dc)*

Rnd 3: Ch 1, (sc, ch 1) in first st,
pc *(see Special Stitch)* in next
st, [dc in next st, pc in next st]
around, join in first dc. *(15 dc,
15 pc)*

Rnd 4: Ch 1, sc in each st
around, join in first sc. *(30 sc)*

Rnds 5–13: Rep rnds 3 and 4
alternately, to desired length to
fit hand, ending with rnd 3.

Rnd 14: Ch 1, [**sc dec** *(see Stitch
Guide)* in next 2 sc] 15 times,
join in first sc. Fasten off.

Sew opening closed. ●

Walker Bag

BY **BELINDA CARTER**

SKILL LEVEL ⬛⬛⬛⬜
INTERMEDIATE

FINISHED SIZE
12 inches wide x 10 inches tall

MATERIALS
- Lion Brand Vanna's Choice medium (worsted) weight yarn (3½ oz/170 yds/100g per ball): 2 balls each #108 dusty and #105 silver blue
- Sizes G/6/4mm and K/10½/6.5mm crochet hooks or size needed to obtain gauge
- Tapestry needle
- Markers

GAUGE
Size K hook: 8 sts = 3 inches; 12 rows = 3 inches

PATTERN NOTES
Weave in loose ends as work progresses.

Join with slip stitch as indicated unless otherwise stated.

SPECIAL STITCHES
Thermal single crochet from front (thermal sc from front): Insert hook in unused front lp of st 2 rows below *(going from bottom to top)* then through front lp of st on row, yo, draw through, yo, draw through both lps on hook.

Thermal single crochet from back (thermal sc from back):

Place yarn in front, insert hook in unused back lp of st 21 rows below *(going from bottom to top)* then through back lp of st on row, yo counterclockwise, draw through, yo counter-clockwise, draw through both lps on hook.

Ending thermal single crochet from front (ending thermal sc from front):

Insert hook in unused front lp of st 2 rows below *(going from bottom to top)* then through both lps of st on row, yo, draw through, yo, draw through both lps on hook.

INSTRUCTIONS

BAG

Row 1 (RS): With size K hook and dusty, work **sc foundation st** *(see Foundation Stitches on page 172)* 32 times, turn, drop lp from hook *(it should look like there is a ch going across the bottom)*. *(32 sc)*

Row 2 (WS): To join silver blue yarn, insert hook in front lp of ch below *(going from bottom to top)* then through front lp of st on row, yo with silver blue, draw through, ch 1, then beg row, [insert hook in front lp of ch below *(going from bottom to top)* then through front lp of st on row, yo, draw through, yo, draw through both lps on hook] 32 times, **do not turn**, drop lp from hook.

Row 3 (WS): Pick up dropped dusty lp, ch 1, work **thermal sc from back** *(see Special Stitches)* in each st across, turn, drop lp from hook.

Row 4 (RS): Pick up dropped silver blue lp, ch 1, work thermal sc from back in each st across, do not turn, drop lp from hook.

Row 5 (RS): Pick up dropped dusty lp, ch 1, work **thermal sc from front** *(see Special Stitches)* in each st across, turn, drop lp from hook.

Row 6 (WS): Pick up dropped silver blue lp, work thermal sc from front in each st across, do not turn, drop lp from hook.

Rep rows 3–6 until piece measures 34 inches, ending with row 4. Fasten off silver blue.

Last row: Pick up dropped dusty lp, ch 1, work **ending thermal sc from front** *(see Special Stitches)* in each st across, **do not turn**.

EDGING

Rnd 1: Ch 1, sc evenly sp around piece, working 3 sc in each corner to turn, join in first sc. Fasten off.

SEWING

Lay piece down with RS facing up. Fold one end upward 6 inches and fold other end upward 8 inches. Sew in place to form pockets.

With size G hook, join dusty to top edge of pocket opening, reverse sc *(Fig. 1)* in each st across pocket. This will draw top of pocket in slightly.

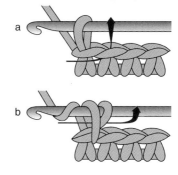

Figure 1
Reverse Single Crochet

Mark off 3 small pockets across the 6-inch tall pocket. Mark first pocket 6 inches wide, mark 2nd pocket 2½ inches wide, and mark 3rd pocket 3½ inches wide. With size K hook and dusty work surface sl st from bottom of pocket to top of pocket, thereby sewing the 6-inch pocket into 3 separate pockets.

POCKET TIE
Make 3.

With size G hook and dusty, ch 60. Fasten off. Attach a Tie to top of smaller pockets at surface sl st seams and the 3rd to center top of larger 8-inch pocket on opposite side. Tie each into a bow.

SIDE TIE
Make 2.

Fold pieces in half. Place a marker 2 inches down from fold on each side front and back. *With size G hook, join dusty at a marker, ch 30. Fasten off. Rep from * for rem 3 markers. Place piece over walker, then tie the Ties on each side to hold in place. ●

Whoa Nellie!

BY **PENNY THOMPSON**

SKILL LEVEL ◖■☐◗
EASY

FINISHED SIZE
Head: 10 inches tall

MATERIALS
- Medium (worsted) weight yarn:
  7 oz black
  1 oz burgundy
- Size I/9/5.5mm crochet hook or size needed to obtain gauge
- Tapestry needle
- Sewing needle
- Black sewing thread
- 2 white ⅞-inch flat buttons
- 2 brass 1-inch rings
- 16 x 32-inch black fabric
- 5-inch square cardboard
- Black electrical tape
- 37-inch long wooden ⅞-inch diameter dowel
- Fiberfill

GAUGE
3 sc = 1 inch; 7 sc rows = 2 inches

PATTERN NOTE
Weave in loose ends as work progresses.

INSTRUCTIONS

HEAD SIDE
Make 2.
Row 1: Starting at nose, with black, work **sc foundation st** *(see Foundation Stitches on page 172)* 5 times, turn. *(5 sc)*

Row 2: Ch 1, 3 sc in first st, sc in each st across to last st, 2 sc in last st, turn. *(8 sc)*

Row 3: Ch 1, 2 sc in first st, sc in each st across to last st, 3 sc in last st, turn. *(11 sc)*

Rows 4 & 5: Rep rows 2 and 3. *(17 sc)*

Row 6: Ch 1, 2 sc in first st, sc in each st across to last st, 2 sc in last st, turn. *(19 sc)*

Row 7: Ch 1, sc in each st across to last st, 2 sc in last st, turn. *(20 sc)*

Row 8: Ch 1, 2 sc in first st, sc in each st across, turn. *(21 sc)*

Row 9: Ch 1, sc in each st across, turn.

Row 10: Ch 1, 2 sc in first st, sc in each st across to last 2 sts, **sc dec** *(see Stitch Guide)* in last 2 sts, turn. *(21 sc)*

Row 11: Ch 1, sc dec in first 2 sts, sc in each st across, turn. *(20 sc)*

Rows 12–15: [Rep rows 10 and 11 alternately] twice.

Row 16: Rep row 10. *(18 sc)*

Rows 17 & 18: Rep row 9.

Row 19: Ch 21 *(for neck)*, sc in 2nd ch from hook, sc in each of next 19 chs, sc in each of next 18 sc, turn. *(38 sc)*

Rows 20–28: Rep row 9.

Row 29: Ch 1, sc in each st across to last 2 sts, sc dec in last 2 sts turn. *(37 sc)*

Row 30: Rep row 9.

Row 31: Rep row 29. *(36 sc)*

Row 32: Rep row 11. *(35 sc)*

Row 33–38: [Rep rows 31 and 32 alternately] 3 times. *(29 sc)*

At the end of row 38, fasten off.

For lining, using one Head Side as pattern, cut 2 pieces from fabric, adding ¼ inch for seam allowance.

Matching sts, with black, sew crocheted Sides tog, leaving neck open.

ASSEMBLY
With RS tog, sew lining pieces

tog, leaving neck open. Turn RS out, press. Place inside Head.

Stuff Head, leaving 2 inches of neck end unstuffed. Insert dowel through center of neck and Head. Wrap tape around neck and dowel.

EAR SIDE
Make 4.
Row 1: With black, work sc foundation st 8 times, turn. *(8 sc)*

Row 2: Ch 1, sc in each st across, turn.

Row 3: Ch 1, sc dec in next 2 sts, sc in each st across to last 2 sts, sc dec in last 2 sts, turn. *(6 sc)*

Rows 4 & 5: Rep rows 2 and 3. *(4 sc)*

Row 6: Rep row 2.

Row 7: Ch 1, [sc dec in next 2 sc] twice, turn. *(2 sc)*

Row 8: Rep row 2. Fasten off.

For each Ear, holding 2 Ear Sides with WS tog, matching sts, with black, sew tog. Sew Ears over top of Head 1 inch apart.

MANE BASE
Row 1: With black, work sc foundation st 24 times, turn. *(24 sc)*

Rows 2 & 3: Ch 1, sc in each st across, turn. At the end of row 3, fasten off.

POMPOM
Make 8.
Wrap black yarn around cardboard 70 times, slide lps off

cardboard; tie separate strand black around middle of all lps. Cut lps and trim ends. Sew Pompoms evenly sp across Base.

Sew Mane across top of Head.

For **eyes**, sew 1 button to each side of Head over row 15.

HALTER
Chin Piece
With burgundy, work **dc foundation st** *(see Foundation Stitches on page 172)* 11 times, fasten off.

Sew 1 ring to each end.

Nose Piece
With burgundy, work dc foundation st 18 times, fasten off.

Sew each end to opposite side of each ring.

Head Piece
Make 2.
With burgundy, work dc foundation st 15 times, fasten off.

Sew 1 end of each piece to top center of each ring between Chin Piece and Nose Piece.

Place Chin Piece and Nose Piece around nose of Head. Pull Head Pieces to top of Head and tack tog beneath Pompoms.

REINS
With burgundy, work dc foundation st 57 times, fasten off.

With Reins hanging over back of dowel, sew ends to center bottom of each ring between Chin Piece and Nose Piece. ●

Gingerbread Checkerboard

BY **JOCELYN SASS**

SKILL LEVEL ■□□□
BEGINNER

FINISHED SIZE
14½ x 20½ inches

MATERIALS
- Medium (worsted) weight yarn:
  - 8 oz brick red
  - 1½ oz each white and red
  - 2 yds black
- Size G/6/4mm crochet hook or size needed to obtain gauge
- Tapestry needle
- Sewing needle
- Matching thread
- Large sheet stiff artist plastic canvas
- 1 yd ⅞-inch-wide red satin ribbon
- 40 inches ⅛-inch-wide white satin ribbon
- 1-inch plastic rings: 2

GAUGE
4 sc = 1 inch; 4 sc rows = 1 inch

PATTERN NOTES
Weave in loose ends as work progresses.

Join with slip stitch as indicated unless otherwise stated.

INSTRUCTIONS

BACK
Row 1 (WS): Starting at bottom with brick red, work **sc foundation st** (see Foundation Stitches on page 172) 52 times, turn. (52 sc)

Rows 2–62: Ch 1, sc in each sc across, turn.

At the end of row 62, fasten off.

HEAD BACK
Row 1: With RS facing, sk first 20 sts of row 62, attach brick red with sc in next sc, sc in each of next 11 sc, turn. (12 sc)

Rows 2–7: Ch 1, 2 sc in first sc, sc in each sc across to last sc, 2 sc in last sc, turn. (24 sc)

Rows 8–17: Ch 1, sc in each sc across, turn.

Rows 18–23: Ch 1, **sc dec** (see Stitch Guide) in next 2 sc, sc in each sc across to last 2 sc, sc dec in last 2 sc, turn. At the end of row 23, **do not turn**. (12 sc at end of last row)

Rnd 24 (RS): Now working in rnds around outer edge, ch 1, sc evenly sp around, working 3 sc in each outer corner, join in first sc. Fasten off.

Note: Using Back as a pattern, cut plastic canvas slightly smaller for inside lining.

FRONT
Row 1 (WS): Starting at bottom with brick red, work sc foundation st 52 times, turn. (52 sc)

Row 2: Ch 1, sc in each sc across, turn.

Rows 3–11: Rep row 2.

Rows 12–52: Following chart and changing colors as indicated in chart, rep row 2. At the end of row 52, fasten off red and white.

Rows 53–62: With brick red, rep row 2. At the end of row 62, fasten off.

HEAD FRONT
Rows 1–23: Rep rows 1–23 of Head Back.

Rnd 24: Rep rnd 24 of Head Back.

CONTINUED ON PAGE 61

Triple Cross Wheelchair Set

BY **TAMMY HILDEBRAND**

SKILL LEVEL ◼◼◻◻
EASY

FINISHED SIZES
Lapghan: 32 inches wide x 58 inches long with 10 inches folded back to form pocket

Tote: 8 inches wide x 8¾ inches high

MATERIALS
- Red Heart Super Saver medium (worsted) weight yarn (7 oz/364 yds/198g per skein):
  2 skeins each #256 carrot (A), #332 ranch red (B), #336 warm brown (C) and #378 claret (D)
- Size J/10/6mm crochet hook or size needed to obtain gauge
- Yarn needle
- Sewing needle
- Matching sewing thread
- 2 leather ⅞-inch shank buttons

GAUGE
12 sts = 4 inches; 11 rows = 4 inches

PATTERN NOTES
Weave in loose ends as work progresses.

Chain-3 at beginning of row counts as first double crochet unless otherwise stated.

SPECIAL STITCH
Triple cross (tr cross): Working over ch-2 sp, around vertical post of skipped st 2 rows previous, yo hook twice, insert hook around 2nd skipped st from front to back, yo, draw lp through, [yo, draw through 2 lps on hook] 3 times, yo hook twice, insert hook around first skipped st from front to back, yo, draw lp through, [yo, draw through 2 lps on hook] 3 times.

INSTRUCTIONS

LAPGHAN
Row 1 (RS): With A, work **dc foundation st** (see Foundation Stitches on page 172) 90 times, turn. (90 dc)

Row 2 (WS): Ch 3 (see Pattern Notes), dc in next st, [ch 2, sk next 2 sts, dc in each of next 2 sts] across. Fasten off, turn. (46 dc, 22 ch-2 sps)

Row 3: Join B with sc in first st, sc in next st, [**tr cross** (see Special Stitch) in next 2 sts, sc in each of next 2 sts] across, turn. (46 dc, 22 tr cross)

Row 4: Rep row 2.

Rows 5 & 6: With C, rep rows 3 and 4, turn.

Rows 7 & 8: With D, rep rows 3 and 4, turn.

Row 9: With A, rep row 3.

Row 10: Rep row 2.

Rows 11–146: [Rep rows 3–10 consecutively] 17 times.

Rows 147–153: Rep rows 3–9.

Row 154: Ch 1, sc in each st across. Fasten off. (90 sc)

SIDE EDGING
Row 1 (RS): Working around post of first st of each row, join A with sc in row 1, sc in each row to end. Fasten off. (154 sc)

Row 2 (RS): Working around post of first st of each row, join A with sc in row 154, sc in each row to end. Fasten off. (154 sc)

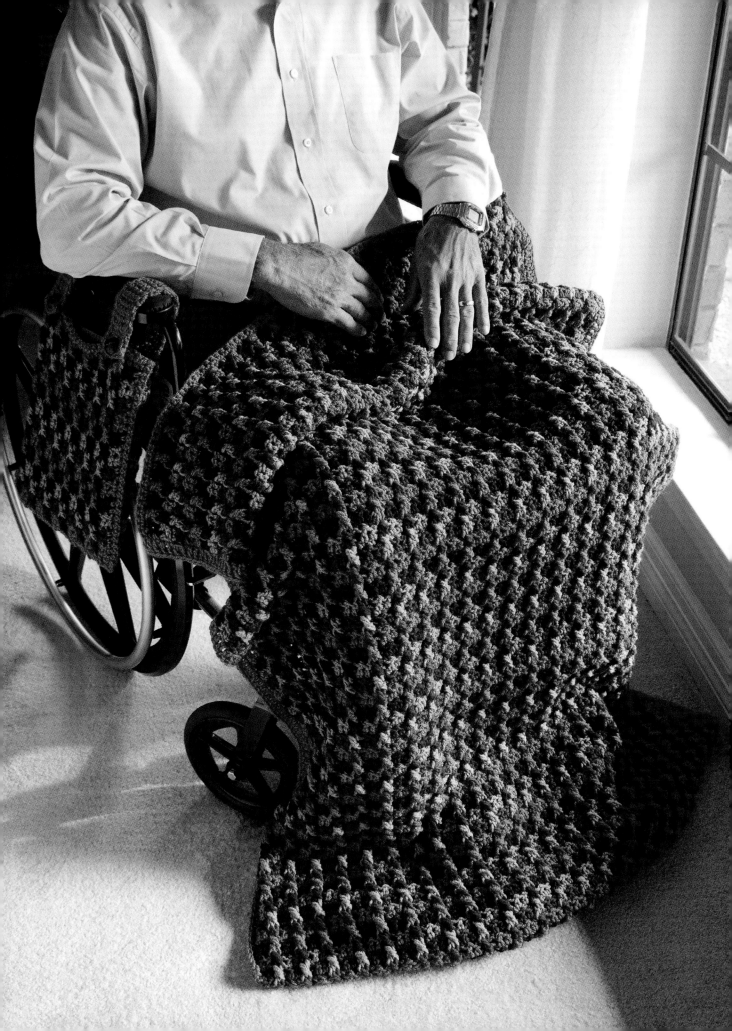

FOOT POCKET
Fold rows 1–26 over rows 27–52. With Pocket facing toward you, matching up sts of Side Edging and working through both thicknesses, join A with sl st in 27th and 28th st at fold, [ch 1, sl st in next st] 25 times. Working in bottom lps of row 1, sl st in each lp across pocket, matching up sts of side edging on opposite side and working through both thicknesses, sl st in next st, [ch 1, sl st in next st] to end. Fasten off.

BORDER
Row 1 (RS): Working in sts of Side Edging and around sl sts of pocket assembly, join A with sl st in first st at fold, ch 3, dc in each st across edge. Fasten off.

Row 2 (RS): Working in sts of Side Edging and around sl sts of pocket assembly, join A with sl st in first st at top, ch 3, dc in each st to fold at bottom edge. Fasten off.

TOTE
FIRST SIDE
Row 1 (RS): With A, work **dc foundation st** (see Foundation Stitches on page 172) 26 times, turn. (26 dc)

Row 2 (WS): Ch 3, dc in next st, [ch 2, sk next 2 sts, dc in each of next 2 sts] across, turn. Fasten off. (14 dc, 6 ch-2 sps)

Row 3: Join B with sc in first st, sc in next st, [**tr cross** (see Special Stitch) over next 2 sts, sc in each of next 2 sts] across, turn. (14 dc, 6 tr cross)

Row 4: Rep row 2.

Rows 5 & 6: With C, rep rows 3 and 4.

Rows 7 & 8: With D, rep rows 3 and 4.

Row 9: With A, rep row 3.

Row 10-18: Rep rows 2-10.

Rows 19–25: Rep rows 3–9.

Row 26: Ch 1, sc in each st across. Fasten off. (26 sc)

2ND SIDE
Row 1: Working in bottom lps of row 1, join A with sl st in first st, ch 3, dc in each st across, turn.

Rows 2–26: Rep rows 2–26 of First Side.

SIDE EDGING
Row 1 (RS): Working around post of first st of each row, join A with sc in row 1, sc in each row across. Fasten off. (52 sc)

Row 2 (RS): Working around post of last st of each row, join A with sc in row 26, sc in each row to opposite edge. Fasten off. (52 sc)

ASSEMBLY
Holding First and 2nd Sides with WS tog, join A with sl st in first st of Side Edging, [ch 1, sl st in next st] across. Fasten off. Join A on opposite edge, rep same on opposite edge.

FIRST HANGER
Row 1: Join A with sc in 4th st of last row on Tote on either side, sc in each of next 4 sts, turn. (5 sc)

Rows 2–18: Ch 1, sc in each st across, turn.

Row 19: Ch 1, sc in each of next 2 sc, ch 2, sk next st (buttonhole), sc in each of next 2 sts, turn. (4 sc, 1 ch-2 sp)

Row 20: Ch 1, sc in each of next 2 sc, sc in ch-2 sp, sc in each of next 2 sc, turn. (5 sc)

Row 21: Ch 1, sc in each of next 4 sc, **do not turn**.

Row 22: Working around post of sts of each row end, ch 1, [sl st in next st, ch 1] across, sl st in same sp as last st of row 1. Fasten off.

Row 23: For opposite edge of same Hanger, join A with sl st in same sp as first st of row 1, [ch 1, sl st in next st] across to last row of Hanger, Fasten off.

2ND HANGER
Row 1: Sk next 10 sts of last row on Tote, join A with sc in next st, sc in each of next 4 sts, turn. (5 sc)

Rows 2–23: Rep rows 2–21 of First Hanger. ●

Slipper Socks

BY **ALINE SUPLINSKAS**

SKILL LEVEL ◼◼◻◻
EASY

FINISHED SIZES
Women's shoe sizes 7–8 [8–9]

MATERIALS
- 3-ply light (light worsted) weight yarn: **3** LIGHT
  - 4 oz burgundy
  - 2 oz tan
- Sizes F/5/3.75mm and G/6/4mm crochet hooks or sizes needed to obtain gauge
- Yarn needle

GAUGES
Size F hook: 5 sc = 1 inch; 5 sc rows = 1 inch

Size G hook: 4 sc = 1 inch; 4 sc rows = 1 inch

PATTERN NOTES
Weave in loose ends as work progresses.

Join with slip stitch as indicated unless otherwise stated.

For extra warmth, the foot is worked with 2 strands of yarn.

INSTRUCTIONS

SOCK CUFF
Make 2.
Row 1: With tan, work **sc foundation st** (see Foundation

Stitches on page 172) 35 times, turn. (35 sc)

Rows 2–44 [46]: Working in **back lp** (see Stitch Guide) of each st, ch 1, sc in each st across, turn. (35 sc)

Row 45 [47]: Fold piece in half, working through both thicknesses of first and last rows, ch 1, sc in each st across, fasten off. Turn RS out.

FOOT
Note: Row 45 [47] is center front.

Row 1: With 2 strands burgundy held tog, attach burgundy in st at end of seam at center front, ch 20 [22] for instep, starting in 2nd ch from hook, sc in each ch across, [sc, ch 1] 17 [18] times evenly sp around Sock Cuff opening, working on opposite side of

CONTINUED ON PAGE 62

Blue Bookmark

BY **SHIRLEY BROWN**

SKILL LEVEL ◖■▢▢
EASY

FINISHED SIZE
14 inches long, including Tassels

MATERIALS
- Size 10 crochet cotton:
  150 yds blue
- Size 2/2.20mm steel
  crochet hook or size
  needed to obtain gauge
- Tapestry needle

GAUGE
2 shells and 1 V-st = 1½ inches

PATTERN NOTES
Weave in loose ends as work progresses.

Chain-2 at beginning of rows does not count as any stitch unless otherwise stated.

SPECIAL STITCHES
Shell: (2 dc, ch 2, 2 dc) in indicated st.

V-stitch (V-st): (Dc, ch 2, dc) in indicated st.

INSTRUCTIONS

BOOKMARK
Row 1: Ch 4, (dc, ch 2, 2 dc)

in 4th ch from hook *(shell completed)* yo 4 times, insert hook in same ch last dc worked in, yo, draw lp through, [yo, draw through 2 lps on hook] 3 times *(3 chs completed)*, yo, draw up 1 lp on hook *(base ch)*, [yo, draw through 2 lps on hook] twice, ch 2, dc in last base ch *(V-st completed)*, yo 4 times, insert hook in same ch as last dc working in, yo, draw

lp through, [yo, draw through 2 lps on hook] 3 times *(3 chs completed)*, yo, draw through 1 lp on hook *(base ch)*, [yo, draw through 2 lps on hook] twice, (dc, ch 2, 2 dc) in last base ch completed, turn. *(2 shells, 1 V-st)*

Row 2: Ch 2 *(see Pattern Notes)*, **V-st** *(see Special Stitches)* in ch sp of first shell, **shell** *(see Special*

CONTINUED ON PAGE 63

Mountain Snow Bookmark

BY **SHIRLEY BROWN**

SKILL LEVEL ■■■□
INTERMEDIATE

FINISHED SIZE
11 inches, including Tassel

MATERIALS
- Size 10 crochet cotton: 150 yds white
- Size 2/2.20mm steel crochet hook or size needed to obtain gauge

GAUGE
Row 1 = 2 inches

PATTERN NOTES
Weave in loose ends as work progresses.

Chain-3 at beginning of row counts as first double crochet unless otherwise stated.

SPECIAL STITCHES
Shell: (2 dc, ch 2, dc in 2nd ch from hook, 2 dc) in place indicated.

Cluster (cl): Ch 3, dc in 3rd ch from hook.

INSTRUCTIONS

BOOKMARK
Row 1: Ch 4, dc in 4th ch from

hook, **yo 4 times, insert hook in same ch last dc worked in, yo, draw lp through, [yo, draw through 2 lps on hook] 3 times *(3 chs completed)*, yo, draw through 1 lp on hook *(base ch)*, [yo, draw through 2 lps on hook] twice *(dc completed)*, (dc, ch 2, dc in 2nd ch from hook, dc) in last base ch *(shell completed)*, yo 4 times, insert hook in same ch last dc worked

in, yo, draw lp through, [yo, draw through 2 lps on hook] 3 times *(3 chs completed)*, *yo, draw through 1 lp on hook *(base ch)*, [yo, draw through 2 lps on hook] twice, rep from * once, rep from ** once, turn. *(6 dc, 2 shells)*

Row 2: Ch 3 *(see Pattern Notes)*, dc in next st, [**cl** *(see Special*

CONTINUED ON PAGE 63

Triple Ripple Baby Afghan

BY **MARTHA MILLER**

SKILL LEVEL ■■■□
INTERMEDIATE

FINISHED SIZE
37 x 42 inches

MATERIALS
- Red Heart Super Saver medium (worsted) weight yarn (solid: 7 oz/364 yds/198g; print: 5 oz/244 yds/141g per skein):
  4 skeins #345 baby print *(A)*
  1 skein each #381 light blue *(B)*, #322 pale yellow *(C)*, #724 baby pink *(D)* and #316 soft white *(E)*
- Size H/8/5mm crochet hook or size needed to obtain gauge
- Tapestry needle

GAUGE
3 dc = 1 inch; 4 dc rows = 2½ inches

PATTERN NOTES
Weave in loose ends as work progresses.

Join with slip stitch as indicated unless otherwise stated.

SPECIAL STITCHES
Foundation 3-double crochet decrease (foundation 3-dc dec): [Yo, insert hook into base of foundation ch just made, yo, draw through st, yo, draw through 1 lp *(base ch)*, yo, draw through 2 lps] 3 times, yo, draw through all 4 lps on hook.

Foundation double crochet shell (foundation dc shell): Work 1 foundation dc, work 2 more dc in base ch just made.

INSTRUCTIONS

AFGHAN
Note: Work Afghan in following stripe sequence: 4 rows A, [2 rows B, 4 rows A, 2 rows C, 4 rows A, 2 rows D, 4 rows A, 2 rows E, 4 rows A] twice.

Row 1 (WS): Starting at bottom edge, with A, ch 4 *(counts as first foundation dc)*, dc in 4th ch from hook, work 3 **dc foundation dc sts** *(see Foundation Stitches on page 172)*, *work **foundation 3-dc dec** *(see Special Stitches)*, work 3 foundation dc sts, work **foundation dc shell** *(see Special Stitches)*, work 3 foundation dc sts, rep from * 10 times, work foundation 3-dc dec, work 5 foundation dc sts, turn.

Row 2 (RS): Ch 3, dc in first st, dc in each of next 3 sts, dc dec in next 3 sts, dc in each of next 3 sts, *3 dc in next st, dc in each of next 3 sts, dc dec in next 3 sts, dc in each of next 3 sts, rep from * across, 2 dc in top of beg ch-3, turn.

Row 3: Ch 3, dc in first dc, dc in each of next 3 dc, dc dec in next 3 sts, dc in each of next 3 dc, *3 dc in next dc, dc in each of next 3 dc, dc dec in next 3 sts, dc in each of next 3 dc, rep from * across, 2 dc in top of beg ch-3, turn.

Rows 4–52: Rep row 3 following stripe sequences. At the end of row 52, fasten off.

BORDER
Note: Work Border with baby pink for a girl and light blue for a boy.

Rnd 1 (RS): Join yarn at bottom left corner with sc, sc in each st through bottom lps of foundation row, 3 sc in corner st, sc evenly sp in ends of rows, 3 sc in corner st, sc across sts of row 52, 3 sc in corner st, sc evenly sp in ends of rows, 3 sc in corner st, join in first sc. Fasten off. ●

Geometric Washcloths

BY **MARTY MILLER**

SKILL LEVEL ■■□□
EASY

FINISHED SIZES
Round: 8 inches in diameter

Square: 8 inches square

Triangle: 9¼ inches across each triangle edge

MATERIALS

- Bernat Handicrafter cotton medium (worsted) weight yarn (solid: 1¾ oz/80 yds/50g; variegated: 1½ oz/68 yds/42g per ball): 1 ball each #13742 hot blue (A), #13712 hot green (B), #00001 white (C), #23743 summer splash (D) and #23713 key lime pie (E)
- Size H/8/5mm crochet hook or size needed to obtain gauge
- Tapestry needle

GAUGE
11 sc = 3 inches; 6 sc rnds = 1½ inches

PATTERN NOTES
Weave in loose ends as work progresses.

Join with slip stitch as indicated unless otherwise stated.

Round 1 establishes the right side of Washcloth.

Each Washcloth gives color variations for each design.

SPECIAL STITCH
Corner stitch (corner st): (Sc, ch 2, sc) in indicated place on previous rnd.

INSTRUCTIONS

ROUND WASHCLOTH
Striped circle: 1 ball each A, B and C. Work 6 rnds A, 5 rnds B and 4 rnds C.

Blue and white circle: 1 ball A and C. Work 2 rnds C, 3 rnds A, 5 rnds C, 3 rnds A and 2 rnds C.

Variegated circle: 1 ball E, rnds 1–15 with E.

Rnd 1 (RS): Starting with a **slip ring foundation st** (see Foundation Stitches on page 172), ch 1, 6 sc in slip ring, join in first sc. (6 sc)

Rnd 2: Ch 1, 2 sc in each sc around, join in first sc. (12 sc)

Rnd 3: Ch 1, 2 sc in first sc, sc in next sc, [2 sc in next sc, sc in next sc] 5 times, join in first sc. (18 sc)

Rnd 4: Ch 1, sc in first sc, 2 sc in next sc, sc in next sc, [sc in next sc, 2 sc in next sc, sc in next sc] 5 times, join in first sc. (24 sc)

Rnd 5: Ch 1, [sc in each of next 3 sc, 2 sc in next sc] 6 times, join in first sc. (30 sc)

Rnd 6: Ch 1, [sc in each of next 2 sc, 2 sc in next sc, sc in each of next 2 sc] 6 times, join in first sc. (36 sc)

Rnd 7: Ch 1, [2 sc in next sc, sc in each of next 5 sc] 6 times, join in first sc. (42 sc)

Rnd 8: Ch 1, [sc in each of next 3 sc, 2 sc in next sc, sc in each of next 3 sc] 6 times, join in first sc. (48 sc)

Rnd 9: Ch 1, [sc in each of next 7 sc, 2 sc in next sc] 6 times, join in first sc. (54 sc)

corner st *(see Special Stitch)* in next sc, [sc in next sc, corner st in next sc] 3 times, join in first sc. *(12 sc, 4 ch-2 sps)*

Rnd 3: Ch 1, sc in each sc around, working corner st in each ch-2 sp, join in first sc. *(20 sc, 4 ch-2 sps)*

Rnd 4: Rep rnd 3. *(28 sc, 4 ch-2 sps)*

Rnd 5: Rep rnd 3. *(36 sc, 4 ch-2 sps)*

Rnds 6–15: Rep rnd 3. *(116 sc, 4 ch-2 sps)*

At the end of rnd 15, fasten off.

TRIANGLE WASHCLOTH
Green and white washcloth: 1 ball each B, C and E. Work 3 rnds B, 1 rnd E, 4 rnds C, 1 rnd E, 5 rnds B and 1 rnd E.

Variegated washcloth: 1 skein D.

Rnd 1 (RS): Starting with a **slip ring foundation st** *(see Foundation Stitches on page 172)*, ch 1, 6 sc in slip ring, join in first sc, ch 1. *(6 sc)*

Rnd 2: Ch 1, [corner st in next sc, sc in next sc] 3 times, join in beg sc. *(9 sc, 3 ch-2 sps)*

Rnd 3: Ch 1, sc in each sc around, working corner st in each ch-2 sp, join in first sc. *(15 sc, 3 ch-2 sps)*

Rnds 4–15: Rep rnd 3. *(87 sc, 3 ch-2 sps)*

At the end of rnd 15, fasten off. ●

Rnd 10: Ch 1, [sc in each of next 4 sc, 2 sc in next sc, sc in each of next 4 sc] 6 times, join in first sc. *(60 sc)*

Rnd 11: Ch 1, [2 sc in next sc, sc in each of next 9 sc] 6 times, join in first sc. *(66 sc)*

Rnd 12: Ch 1, [sc in each of next 5 sc, 2 sc in next sc, sc in each of next 5 sc] 6 times, join in first sc. *(72 sc)*

Rnd 13: Ch 1, [sc in each of next 11 sc, 2 sc in next sc] 6 times, join in first sc. *(78 sc)*

Rnd 14: Ch 1, [sc in each of next 6 sc, 2 sc in next sc, sc in each of next 6 sc] 6 times, join in first sc. *(84 sc)*

Rnd 15: Ch 1, [2 sc in next sc, sc in each of next 13 sc] 6 times, join in first sc. Fasten off. *(90 sc)*

SQUARE WASHCLOTH
Striped washcloth: 1 ball each A and D. Work 1 rnd A, 1 rnd D, 2 rnds A, 1 rnd D, 1 rnd A, 1 rnd D, 2 rnds A, 1 rnd D, 2 rnds A, 1 rnd D, 1 rnd A and 1 rnd D.

Green and white washcloth: 1 ball each B, C, and E. Work 5 rnds E, 3 rnds C, 2 rnds E and 5 rnds B.

Rnd 1 (RS): Starting with a **slip ring foundation st** *(see Foundation Stitches on page 172)*, ch 1, 8 sc in slip ring, join in first sc. *(8 sc)*

Rnd 2: Ch 1, sc in first sc,

Ribbed Tote Bag

BY **MARTHA MILLER**

SKILL LEVEL
INTERMEDIATE

FINISHED SIZE
8½ x 10 inches, excluding Handle

MATERIALS

- Lily Sugar 'n Cream medium (worsted) weight yarn (2½ oz/120 yds/70g per ball):
  4 balls #00083 cornflower blue
- Size H/8/5mm crochet hook or size needed to obtain gauge
- Tapestry needle

GAUGE
3 sc = 1 inch; 7 sc rows = 2 inches

PATTERN NOTES
Weave in loose ends as work progresses.

Join rounds with slip stitch as indicated unless otherwise stated.

Tote is worked in rounds on the right side only. Do not turn rounds.

INSTRUCTIONS

TOTE
Foundation row: Starting at bottom, ch 3 *(counts as a foundation dc)*, work **dc founda-**

tion st *(see Foundation Stitches on page 172)* 29 times *(30 dc)*, turn this foundation row upside down, to work sts in the bottom lps of each foundation base ch of each foundation dc, dc in each bottom st across, join in top of first ch-3. *(30 foundation dc, 30 dc)*

Rnd 1 (RS): Ch 2 *(counts as first bpdc)*, sk first ch-3 in previous rnd, **bpdc** *(see Stitch Guide)* around each of next 4 dc, **fpdc** *(see Stitch Guide)* around each of next 5 dc, [bpdc around each of next 5 dc, fpdc around each of next 5 dc] around, join in 2nd ch of first ch-2.

Rnd 2: Ch 2, sk first ch-2 sp of previous rnd, bpdc around each

of next 4 bpdc, fpdc around next 5 fpdc, [bpdc around each of next 5 bpdc, fpdc around each of next 5 fpdc] around, join in 2nd ch of first ch-2.

Rnds 3–30: Rep rnd 2. At the end of rnd 30, turn, working in front lps only, sl st in each of next 6 sts, turn.

HANDLE

Row 1 (RS): Ch 2 *(counts as first hdc)*, fpdc around each of next 5 fpdc, bpdc around each of next 5 bpdc, hdc in next st, turn.

Row 2: Ch 2, fpdc around each of next 5 fpdc, bpdc around each of next 5 dc, hdc in top of beg ch-2, turn.

Rows 3–30: Rep row 2.

Row 31: Ch 2, bpdc around each of next 5 fpdc, fpdc around each of next 5 bpdc, hdc in top of beg ch-2, turn.

Rows 32–60: Ch 2, bpdc around each of next 5 bpdc, fpdc around each of next 5 fpdc, hdc in top of beg ch-2, turn.

Row 61: With RS of Tote and Handle held tog, matching sts on opposite side of Tote Bag from beg of Handle, ch 1, working through both thicknesses, sc in each of next 12 sts. Fasten off. ●

Cabled Dog Set CONTINUED FROM PAGE 37

Row 7: Fpdc around next st, dc in each of next 2 sts, pc in next st, dc in each of next 2 sts, cross cable, dc in each of next 2 sts, pc in next st, dc in each of next 2 sts, fpdc around next st.

Row 8: Bpdc around next st, dc in each of next 5 sts, bpdc around each of next 2 sts, dc in next st, bpdc around each of next 2 sts, dc in each of next 5 sts, bpdc around next st.

Row 9: Fpdc around next st, dc in each of next 5 sts, fpdc around each of next 2 sts, dc in next st, fpdc around each of next 2 sts, dc in each of next 5 sts, fpdc around next st.

Row 10: Bpdc around next st, dc in each of next 5 sts, bpdc around each of next 2 sts, dc in next st, bpdc around each of next 2 sts, dc in each of next 5 sts, bpdc around next st.

INSTRUCTIONS

SWEATER
BODY
Row 1: Starting at back bottom edge, ch 3 *(counts as first dc)*, **dc foundation st** *(see Foundation Stitches on page 172)* 36 [38, 40] times, turn. *(37 [39, 41] dc)*

Row 2: Ch 3, dc in same st as first dc, *dc in each of next 5 sts, **bpdc** *(see Stitch Guide)* around each of next 2 sts, dc in next st, bpdc around each of next 2 sts, dc in each of next 5 sts*, bpdc around next st, dc in each of next 3 [5, 7] sts, bpdc around next st, rep from * to *, 2 dc in last st, turn. *(39 [41, 43] sts)*

Row 3: Ch 3, dc in same st as first dc, work row 3 of Cable Pattern, dc in each of next 3 [5, 7] sts, rep same row 3 of Cable Pattern, 2 dc in last st, turn. *(41 [43, 45] sts)*

Row 4: Ch 3, dc in same st as first dc, dc in next st, work row 4 of Cable Pattern, dc in each of next 3 [5, 7] sts, rep row 4 of Cable Pattern, dc in next st, 2 dc in last st, turn. *(43 [45, 47] sts)*

Rows 5–12 [5–14, 5–16]: Ch 3, dc in same st, dc in each st across to next post st, work next row of Cable Pattern, dc in each of next 3 [5, 7] sts, rep same row of Cable Pattern, dc in each st across, with 2 dc in last st, turn. *(59 [65, 71] sts)*

Rows 13 & 14 [15 & 16, 17 & 18]: Ch 3, dc in each st across to next post st, work next row of Cable Pattern, dc in each of next 3 [5, 7] sts, rep same row of Cable Pattern, dc in each st across, turn.

LEG OPENINGS
Row 1 (Right edge): Ch 3, dc in each of next 3 [4, 5] sts, leaving rem sts unworked, turn. *(4 [5, 6] sts)*

Row 2: Sc, ch 1 in first st *(not counted as a st)*, dc in each st across, turn. *(3 [4, 5] sts)*

Rows 3–6: Ch 3, dc in each st across, turn. At the end of last rep, fasten off. *(3 [4, 5] sts)*

Row 1 (Back section): Sk next 2 sts on Row 14 [16, 18] for leg opening, join with sc in next

st, ch 2 *(counts as first dc)*, dc in each st across to next post st, work next row of Cable Pattern, dc in each of next 3 [5, 7] sts, rep same row of Cable Pattern, dc in each st across to last 6 [7, 8] sts, leaving rem sts unworked, turn. *(43 [47, 51] sts)*

Rows 2–5: Ch 3, dc in each st across to next post st, work next row of Cable Pattern, dc in each of next 3 [5, 7] sts, rep same row of Cable Pattern, dc in each st across, turn. At the end of last row, fasten off.

Note: Back section has one less row than side sections.

Row 1 (Left side): Sk next 2 sts on row 14 [16, 18] for Leg Opening, join with sc in next st, ch 2 *(counts as first dc)*, dc in each st across, turn. *(4 [5, 6] sts)*

Row 2: Ch 3, dc in each st across to last 2 sts, **dc dec** *(see Stitch Guide)* in next 2 sts, turn. *(3 [4, 5] sts)*

Rows 3–6: Ch 3, dc in each st across, turn. At the end of row 6, fasten off.

NECK
Row 1: With WS facing, working across all sections, join yarn with sc in first st on first side, ch 2 *(counts as first dc)*, dc in each of next 1 [2, 3] st(s), work **dc joining** *(see Special Stitches)*, dc again into same first st on back section (beside dc joining), dc across to 3 sts before next post st, dc dec in next 2 sts, dc in next st, work next row of Cable

Pattern, ch 1, sl st in each of next 3 [5, 7] sts, ch 1, rep same row of Cable Pattern, dc in next st, dc dec in next 2 sts, dc in each st across back section to last st, work dc joining, dc again into same first st on left side, dc in each st across, turn. *(51 [57, 63] sts)*

Row 2: Ch 3, dc in each of next 1 [3, 3] st(s), [dc dec in next 2 sts] twice, dc in each st across to next post st, *fpdc, dc dec in next 2 sts, pc in next st, dc dec in next 2 sts, **cross cable** (see Special Stitches), dc dec in next 2 sts, pc in next st, dc dec in next 2 sts, fpdc*, sk ch-1 and working over sl sts, dc in each of next 3 [5, 7] sts on previous row, rep from * to *, dc across to last 6 [8, 8] sts, [dc dec in next 2 sts] twice, dc in each of last 4 sts, turn. *(39 [45, 51] sts)*

Row 3: Ch 3, dc in each st across to next post st, *bpdc around next st, dc in each of next 3 sts, bpdc around each of next 2 sts, dc in next st, bpdc around each of next 2 sts, dc in each of next 3 sts, bpdc around next st*, dc in each of next 3 [5, 7] sts, rep from * to *, dc in each st across, turn.

Row 4: Ch 3, dc in each st across to next post st, *fpdc around next st, dc in each of next 3 sts, fpdc around each of next 2 sts, dc in next st, fpdc around each of next 2 sts, dc in each of next 3 sts, fpdc around next st*, sc in each of next 3 [5, 7] sts *(sc sts are center back neck)*, rep from * to *, dc in each st across, turn, **do not fasten off.**

COLLAR
Row 1: With WS facing, ch 1, sc in first st, work 4 **foundation sc sts** (see Foundation Stitches on page 172), ch 1, working in **back lps** (see Stitch Guide) of base chs, (sl st, ch 1, sc) in first ch, sc in each of next 3 chs, sc in both lps of each of next 2 unworked sts on row 4 of Neck, turn. (6 sc)

Row 2: Sk first 2 sc, sc in back lps of each of next 4 sts, turn. (4 sc)

Row 3: Ch 1, sc in back lps of each of next 4 sts, sc in both lps of each of next 2 unworked sts on row 4, turn.

Rep rows 2 and 3 alternately, ending with row 3. At the end of last rep, sl st in last st on row 4 of Neck. Fasten off.

EDGING
Note: Mark positions for 4 buttonholes evenly sp at end of rows across right edge with first buttonhole on row 14 [16, 18] and last buttonhole on last row before Collar.

Row 1: With RS facing, join yarn with sc in base of foundation dc at right end of row 1 of Body, evenly sp 2 sc in end of each row across with last sc in top of st on row 14 [16, 18], ch 5 (for buttonhole), sc in next row, [evenly sp 2 sc in end of each row across to next marker, ch 4, sc in next row] across, sl st in first sc on Collar. Fasten off.

Row 2: With RS facing, join yarn with sc in top of last st on row 4 of neck on left side, evenly sp 2 sc in end of each row across with 2 sc in top of st on row 14 [16, 18] and ending with last sc in ch-1 at base of foundation dc on row 1. Fasten off.

Using sewing needle and thread, sew buttons opposite buttonholes.

LEG TRIM
Make 2.
Rnd 1 (RS): Join yarn with sc in first sk st on row 14 [16, 18], ch 2 (counts as first dc), dc in next st, evenly sp 2 dc in end of each row around, **join** (see Pattern Notes) in first dc.

Row 2: Now working in rows, ch 1, sc in first st, 4 foundation sc sts, **do not turn.** (5 sc)

Row 3: Ch 1, working in back lps of chs at base of foundation sts, (sl st, ch 1, sc) in ch at base of last sc made, sc in each of next 3 chs, sc in both lps of each of next 2 unworked sts on rnd 1, turn. (6 sc)

Row 4: Sk first 2 sc, sc in back lps of each of next 4 sts, turn. (4 sc)

Row 5: Ch 1, sc in back lps of each of next 4 sts, sc in both lps of each of next 2 unworked sts on rnd 1, turn.

Rep rows 4 and 5 alternately around leg opening, ending with row 4.

Last row: Ch 1, sc in back lps of each of next 4 sts, sc in both lps of last unworked st on rnd

1. Leaving 12-inch length for sewing, fasten off.

With WS tog, sew inside lps of first and last rows tog, forming a matching ridge.

BOOT
Make 4.
Rnd 1: Ch 3, 2 sc in 2nd ch from hook, 4 sc in last ch, working on opposite side of foundation ch, 2 sc in next ch, join in first sc. (8 sc)

Rnd 2: Ch 1, 2 sc in first sc, sc in each of next 2 sc, 2 sc in each of next 2 sc, sc in each of next 2 sc, 2 sc in last sc, **join** (see Pattern Notes) in first sc. (12 sc)

Rnd 3: Ch 1, 2 sc in each of next 2 sc, sc in each of next 3 sc, 2 sc in each of next 3 sc, sc in each of next 3 sc, 2 sc in last sc, join in beg sc. (18 sc)

Rnd 4: Ch 1, **bpsc** (see Stitch Guide) in each st around, join.

Rnd 5: Ch 1, sc in each of first 5 sts, [**hdc-sc dec** (see Special Stitches) in next 2 sts] twice, dc in next st (center front), [hdc-sc dec in next 2 sts] twice, sc in next 4 sts, join in beg sc. (14 sc)

Rnd 6: Ch 1, hdc in same st as beg ch-1, hdc in each st around, join in first hdc. (14 hdc)

Rnd 7: Ch 1, sc in first st, ch 1, sk next st, [sc in next st, ch 1, sk next st] 6 times, join in beg sc, **do not fasten off.** (7 ch-1 sps)

RIBBING
Note: Work ribbing on each Boot.

Row 1: Ch 1, sc in first st of rnd 7, work 4 **foundation sc sts** *(see Foundation Stitches on page 172)*, **do not turn.** *(5 sc)*

Row 2: Working in back lps of chs at base of foundation sts, (sl st, ch 1, sc) in ch at base of last sc made, sc in each of next 3 chs, sc in next ch sp on rnd 7, sc in both lps of next unworked st, turn. *(6 sc)*

Row 3: Sk first 2 sc, sc in back lps of each of next 4 sts, turn. *(4 sc)*

Row 4: Ch 1, sc in back lps of each of next 4 sts, sc in next ch sp on rnd 7, sc in both lps of next unworked st, turn.

Rep rows 3 and 4 alternately around, ending with row 3.

Last row: Ch 1, sc in back lps of each of next 4 sts, sc in last ch sp on rnd 7. Leaving a length of yarn, fasten off.

TIE
Make 4.
Make a ch to measure 10 inches. Fasten off. Weave in ends.

Starting at center front, weave Tie through ch-1 sps of rnd 7 of Boot, tie in a bow at center front. ●

Gingerbread Checkerboard CONTINUED FROM PAGE 44

Fig. 1
Satin Stitch

Fig. 2
Straight Stitch

EYES
Using photo as a guide, embroider black satin st *(Fig. 1)* Eyes 2 inches apart over rows 16 and 17.

MOUTH
Using photo as a guide, embroider red straight st *(Fig. 2)* Mouth over rows 7–11.

JOINING
Hold Front and Back tog with plastic canvas sandwiched between. With length of brick red, working in **back lps** *(see Stitch Guide)*, sew sections tog.

CHECKERS
Make 12 each white and red.
Rnd 1: Slip ring *(see Foundation Stitches on page 172)*, ch 1, 8 sc in ring, join in first sc. Fasten off.

HANGING RINGS
Make 2.
Attach red to plastic ring, ch 1, sc over ring until covered, join in first sc. Leaving 12-inch length of yarn, fasten off.

Sew a ring to each side at top Back.

FINISHING
String Checkers onto white satin ribbon. Lp each end of white satin ribbon through Hanging Rings and tie into a bow. Untie one side to use Checkers. Tie red satin ribbon in bow and sew to side of Head. ●

GRAPH ON PAGE 62

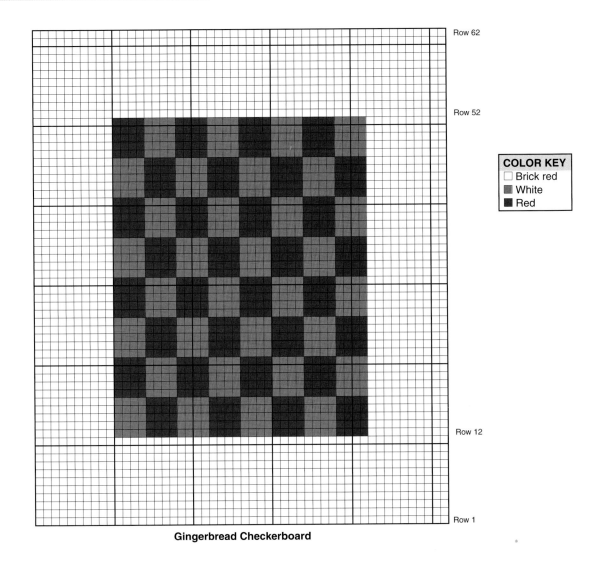

Row 62

Row 52

COLOR KEY
☐ Brick red
▨ White
■ Red

Row 12

Row 1

Gingerbread Checkerboard

Slipper Socks CONTINUED FROM PAGE 49

foundation ch, sc in each ch across, turn.

Row 2: Working in back lps only, ch 1, sc in each sc and each ch-1 sp across Foot, turn.

Rows 3–17: Working in back lps only, ch 1, sc in each st across, turn.

Row 18: Turn Slipper WS out, fold piece in half evenly and

working through both thicknesses, sc in each st across, leaving a length of yarn. Fasten off.

Turn Slipper RS out. With yarn needle and rem length, gather across toe sts, draw opening closed, secure and fasten off.

TIE
Make 2.
Note: *Pattern offers two options*

for Ties. Twisted Cord Ties or Chain Ties.

Twisted Cord Tie

Cut 2 strands of each tan and burgundy 85 inches long.

Have someone hold ends, while from opposite end you twist all yarns tog. Fold in half and while holding all ends tog, let strands twist themselves; make a knot. With the folded end, starting at center front, weave through ch-1 sps of row 1 of Foot, after weave is completed, make a knot in this end also and trim both ends evenly. Tie ends in a bow.

Chain Tie

Cut 2 strands of each tan and burgundy 85 inches long. With size F hook, holding strands tog, ch across. ●

Blue Bookmark CONTINUED FROM PAGE 50

Stitches) in ch sp of next V-st, V-st in ch sp of last shell, turn.

Row 3: Ch 2, shell in ch sp of first V-st, V-st in ch sp of next shell, shell in ch sp of next V-st, turn.

Rows 4–19: [Rep rows 2 and 3 alternately] 8 times. At the end of row 19, fasten off.

CENTER CHAIN

Leaving a 4-inch length at beg, make a ch 8 inches long. Leaving a 4-inch length, fasten off.

Leaving approximately 6 chs each, top and bottom, weave chain through center ch sps of Bookmark.

TASSEL
Make 2.
Wrap blue around 4 fingers 20 times. Tie separate strand through center of strands. Cut ends.

Wrap separate strand several times around all the strands ½-inch below first tie.

Attach 1 Tassel to each end of Center Chain. ●

Mountain Snow Bookmark CONTINUED FROM PAGE 51

Stitches), ch 1, cl, sk first dc of shell, dc in each of next 2 dc] twice, turn.

Row 3: Ch 3, dc in next st, [**shell** (see Special Stitches) in ch-1 between cls, dc in each of next 2 dc] twice, turn.

Rows 4–21: [Rep rows 2 and 3 alternately] 9 times.

Row 22: Ch 3, dc in next st, cl, sk dc of shell, 2 tr in next dc, ch 5, sl st in 5th ch from hook, ch 7, sl st in 7th ch from hook, ch 5, sl st in 5th ch from hook, 2 tr in next dc, cl, dc in each of last 2 dc. Fasten off.

TASSEL
Wind yarn around 2 fingers 50 times. Tie separate strand through center of strands. Cut ends. Wrap separate strand several times around all the strands ½-inch below first tie.

FINISHING
Join with sl st in bottom center dc on opposite side of row 1, ch 10, sl st in top of Tassel. Fasten off.

Join with sl st in bottom of first dc on opposite side of row 1, ch 12, sl st in top of Tassel. Fasten off.

Join with sl st in bottom of first dc on opposite side of row 1 (opposite previous ch-12), sl st in top of Tassel, Fasten off. ●

Around the House

Chapter Contents

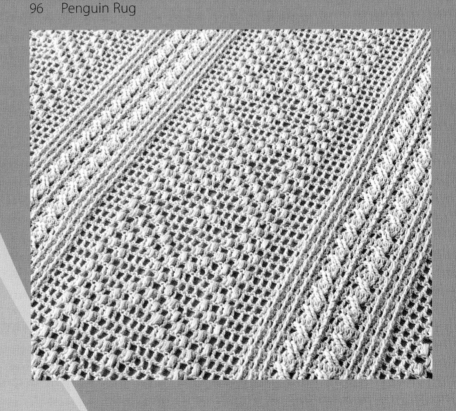

Rectangular Granny Afghan

BY **MARTY MILLER**

SKILL LEVEL ■■□□
EASY

FINISHED SIZE
50 x 55 inches

MATERIALS
- Lion Brand Homespun bulky (chunky) weight yarn (6 oz/185 yds/170g per skein): **5 BULKY**
    1 skein each #322 baroque (A), #393 cream (B), #371 Boston rose (C), #380 fawn (D), #386 grape (E), #394 golden (F), #397 russet (G), and #370 coral gables (H)
- Size K/10½/6.5mm crochet hook or size needed to obtain gauge
- Yarn needle

GAUGE
3 dc = 1 inch; 2 dc rnds = 2 inches

PATTERN NOTES
Weave in loose ends as work progresses.

Join with slip stitch as indicated unless otherwise stated.

At the end of each round, fasten off yarn, join next color in following color sequence:

[A, B, C, D, E, F, G, H] 4 times.

Round 1 establishes the right side of Afghan; do not turn rounds.

SPECIAL STITCHES
Corner: [3 dc, ch 1] twice in indicated st or sp.

Beginning corner (beg corner): (Ch 3, 2 dc, ch 1, 3 dc, ch 1) in indicated st or sp.

INSTRUCTIONS

AFGHAN
Rnd 1 (RS): With A, working **dc eyelet** (*see Foundation Stitches on page 172*) work **beg corner** (*see Special Stitches*), **corner** (*see Special Stitches*) in same eyelet sp, (3 dc, ch 1) in next eyelet sp, (3 dc, ch 1) 4 times in next eyelet sp (*2 corners completed*). Now working in opposite side of dc eyelet, (3 dc, ch 1) in next eyelet sp, **join** (*see Pattern Notes*) in 3rd ch of beg ch. Fasten off.

Rnd 2: Join B in next ch-1 sp, beg corner in same ch-1 sp, (3 dc, ch 1) in next ch-1 sp, corner in next ch-1 sp, (3 dc, ch 1) in each of next 2 ch-1 sps, corner

in next ch-1 sp, (3 dc, ch 1) in next ch-1 sp, corner in next ch-1 sp, (3 dc, ch 1) in each of next 2 ch-1 sps, join in 3rd ch of beg ch. Fasten off.

Rnd 3: Join C in next ch-1 sp, beg corner in same ch-1 sp, (3 dc, ch 1) in each of next 2 ch-1 sps, corner in next ch-1 sp, (3 dc, ch 1) in each of next 3 ch-1 sps, corner in next ch-1 sp, (3 dc, ch 1) in each of next 2 ch-1 sps, corner in next ch-1 sp, (3 dc, ch 1) in each of next 3 ch-1 sps, join in 3rd ch of beg ch. Fasten off.

Rnd 4: Join D in next ch-1 sp, beg corner in same ch-1 sp, (3 dc, ch 1) in each of next 3 ch-1 sps, corner in next ch-1 sp, (3 dc, ch 1) in each of next 4 ch-1 sps, corner in next ch-1 sp, (3 dc, ch 1) in each of next 3 ch-1 sps, corner in next ch-1 sp, (3 dc, ch 1) in each of next 4 ch-1 sps, join in 3rd ch of beg ch. Fasten off.

Rnds 5–32: Continue as established, changing color each rnd to maintain color sequence (*see Pattern Notes*) and inc a 3-dc group each rnd on each side and each end of Afghan between corners. ●

Winter Warmer Throw

BY **KATHERINE ENG**

SKILL LEVEL ■■■□
INTERMEDIATE

FINISHED SIZE
45 x 55 inches

MATERIALS

- N. Y. Yarns Olympic medium (worsted) weight yarn (1¾ oz/130 yds/50g per ball):
    7 balls #01 cream
    5 balls each #06 sky blue and #07 cadet blue
- Size I/9/5.5mm crochet hook or size needed to obtain gauge
- Tapestry needle

GAUGE
4 sc and 3 ch-1 sps across on row 1 = 2 inches; Rows 1–6 = 2½ inches 4 sc and 3 ch-1 sps across on row 1 = 2 inches

PATTERN NOTES
Weave in loose ends as work progresses.

Join with slip stitch as indicated unless otherwise stated.

Throw is crocheted vertically from center foundation ch outward on each side.

SPECIAL STITCH
Shell: 3 dc in indicated st.

INSTRUCTIONS

THROW FIRST HALF
Foundation row: Starting at center with cream, **back bar sc foundation st** *(see Foundation Stitches on page 172)* 95 times, turn. *(95 sc)*

Row 1 (RS): Ch 1, sc in first sc, [ch 1, sk next ch-1 lp, sc in next sc] across, turn. *(95 sc, 94 ch-1 sps)*

Row 2: Ch 1, sc in first sc, [ch 3, sk next 3 sts *(ch-1 sp, sc and ch-1 sp)*, sc in next sc] across, turn. *(47 ch-3 sps, 48 sc)*

Row 3: Ch 1, sc in first sc, [**shell** *(see Special Stitch)* in next ch-3 sp, sc in next sc] across, turn. *(47 shells, 48 sc)*

Row 4: Ch 4 *(counts as first dc, ch-1)*, sc in center dc of shell, ch 1, dc in next sc, [ch 1, sc in center dc of next shell, ch 1, dc in next sc] across, turn. *(48 dc, 47 sc)*

Row 5: Ch 1, sc in first dc, [ch 1, sk next ch-1 sp, sc in next sc, ch 1, sk next ch-1 sp, sc in next dc]

across, turn. *(95 sc, 94 ch-1 sps)*

Row 6: Rep row 2.

Row 7 (RS): With cadet blue, draw up a lp in first sc, rep row 3.

Rows 8–10: Rep rows 4–6.

Rows 11–14: With sky blue, rep rows 3–6.

Rows 15–18: With cadet blue, rep rows 3–6.

Rows 19–30: With cream, [rep rows 3–6 consecutively] 3 times.

Rows 31–42: Rep rows 7–18.

Rows 43–54: Rep rows 19–30. At the end of row 54, fasten off.

THROW 2ND HALF
Row 1 (RS): Working on opposite side of Foundation row, draw up a lp of cream in first sc, rep row 1.

Rows 2–54: Rep rows 2–54 of Throw First Half.

BORDER
Rnd 1 (RS): Working on either

long side edge, draw up a lp of cadet blue in 2nd sc to the left of corner sc, ch 1, *working across long edge, work row 3 of Throw across, (sc, shell, sc) in corner sc; working across short edge, [sk 1 row, shell in end of next row, sc in end of next row] 17 times, shell in end of next row, sc in center sc, [shell in end of next row, sk 1 row, sc in end of next row] 17 times, shell in end of next row,

sk next row, (sc, shell, sc) in next corner sc *(36 shells across between corner shells)*, rep from * across rem 2 sides, **join** *(see Pattern Notes)* in beg sc.

Rnd 2 (RS): *Ch 1, (sc, ch 2, sc) in center dc of next shell, ch 1, sl st in next sc, rep from * around working at each corner (sc, ch 2, sc) in each dc, sl st in next sc, at end of rnd, sl st in joining sl st of last rnd. Fasten off.

Rnd 3 (WS): Draw up a lp of sky blue in any ch-2 sp away from corner, ch 1, sc in same ch-2 sp, [ch 3, sc in next ch-2 sp] rep around, working at each corner ch-2 sp, ch 3, (sc, ch 3, sc), join in beg sc, turn.

Rnd 4: Ch 1, sc in same sc, shell in each ch-3 sp and sc in each sc around, join with last shell in beg sc. Fasten off. ●

Ribbed Throw

BY ELLEN GORMLEY

SKILL LEVEL ◼◼◻◻
EASY

FINISHED SIZE
48 x 56 inches

MATERIALS
- Red Heart Light & Lofty super bulky (super chunky) weight yarn (6 oz/140 yds/170g per skein): 10 skeins #9334 café au lait
- Size M/13/9mm crochet hook or size needed to obtain gauge
- Yarn needle

GAUGE
8 dc = 4 inches; 6 rows = 4 inches

PATTERN NOTE
Weave in loose ends as work progresses.

INSTRUCTIONS

THROW
Row 1: Starting at bottom edge, work **dc foundation st** *(see Foundation Stitches on page 172)* 95 times, turn. *(95 dc)*

Row 2: Ch 3 *(counts as first dc)*, dc in each of next 2 dc, [**fpdc** *(see Stitch Guide)* in next st, dc in next st] 45 times, dc in each of last 2 dc, turn. *(95 sts)*

Row 3: Ch 3, dc in each of next 2 dc, [**bpdc** *(see Stitch Guide)* in

next st, dc in next st] 45 times, dc in each of last 2 dc, turn. *(95 sts)*

Rows 4–71: [Rep rows 2 and 3 alternately] 34 times.

Row 72: Rep row 2.

Row 73: Ch 3, dc in each of next 94 sts, **do not fasten off**.

EDGING
Note: Edging is worked on 3 sides only.

Row 74 (RS): Working down left long edge of Throw, ch 1, 2 sc in side of each of next 73 dc *(146 sc)*, working across bottom edge, ch 3, dc in each of next 93 sts across row 1 foundation edge, ch 3 *(counts as last dc)*, working up right long edge of project, ch 1, 2 sc in side edge of each of next 73 dc *(146 sc)*. Fasten off. *(292 sc, 95 dc)* ●

Idaho Country Bed Spread

BY **JOYCE NORDSTROM**

SKILL LEVEL ⬛⬛⬛⬜
INTERMEDIATE

FINISHED SIZE
Full size: 76 x 81 inches, including Border

Queen size: 89 x 99 inches, including Border

MATERIALS
- Aunt Lydia's Fashion Crochet size 3 crochet cotton (150 yds per ball): 55 [67] balls #226 natural
- Size E/4/3.5mm crochet hook or size needed to obtain gauge
- Yarn needle

GAUGES
10 open blocks = 4 inches; 9 rows = 4 inches

Panel = approximately 13 inches wide

PATTERN NOTES
Weave in loose ends as work progresses.

Join with slip stitch as indicated unless otherwise stated.

SPECIAL STITCHES
Beginning opening block

(beg open bl): Ch 4 *(counts as first dc, ch 1)*, sk next st, dc in next st.

Open block (open bl): Ch 1, sk next st, dc in next st.

Cluster (cl): Retaining all lps on hook, (yo, insert hook in ch sp, yo, draw up a lp) 4 times in same sp, yo, draw through all 9 lps on hook, ch 1 to lock.

Cable twist: Sk next 2 sts, fptr around each of next 2 sts, fptr around first sk st, fptr around 2nd sk st.

Open block decrease (open bl dec): Retaining all lps on hook and sk ch-1 sp, [yo, draw up a lp in next dc, yo, draw through 2 lps on hook] twice, yo, draw through all 3 lps on hook.

INSTRUCTIONS

PANEL
Make 5 [6].
Foundation row (RS): Starting at bottom, work **dc foundation st** *(see Foundation Stitches on page 172)* 55 times, turn. *(55 dc)*

Row 1: Ch 3 *(counts as first dc)*, dc in each dc across, turn.

Row 2 (RS): Ch 3, dc in next dc, **cable twist** *(see Special Stitches)* in next 4 sts, [dc in next st, **fptr** *(see Stitch Guide)* in next st] 3 times, dc in next st *(right edge Panel border)*, follow chart across next 21 sps of row, [fptr in next st, dc in next st] 3 times, cable twist in next 4 sts, dc in each of next 2 sts *(left edge Panel border)*, turn.

Row 3 (WS): Ch 3, dc in each of next 12 sts across border, follow chart across next 21 sps of rows, dc in each of next 13 sts across border, turn.

Keeping the 13 border sts at beg and end of each row, rep rows 2 and 3 as indicated by chart.

JOINING
With RS facing, match sides of 2 Panels. Attach cotton at end, working from left to right through both thicknesses, [ch 1, sc in next row end] across. Fasten off; join rem Panels in same manner.

CONTINUED ON PAGE 106

Garden Bath Set

BY **GLENDA WINKLEMAN**

SKILL LEVEL ◼◼◼◻
INTERMEDIATE

FINISHED SIZES
Rug: 24 x 31 inches

Seat cover: 13½ x 15 inches

Bathroom tissue cover: 6¼ inches in diameter x 5½ inches high

MATERIALS
- TLC Essentials medium (worsted) weight yarn  (6 oz/312 yds/170g per skein):
  - 3 skeins #2316 winter white *(A)*
  - 2 skeins #2772 light country rose *(B)*
  - 1 skein #2672 light thyme *(C)*
  - 2 oz #2220 butter *(D)*
- Sizes J/10/6mm and K/10½/6.5mm crochet hooks or sizes needed to obtain gauge
- Yarn needle
- Stitch marker

GAUGES
Size J hook and 1 strand of yarn held tog: 13 sc = 4 inches; 15 rows = 4 inches

Size K hook and 2 strands of yarn held tog: 10 sc = 4 inches; 12 sc rows = 4 inches

PATTERN NOTES
Weave in loose ends as work progresses.

Join with slip stitch as indicated unless otherwise stated.

SPECIAL STITCHES
Cluster (cl): Yo, insert hook in indicated st, yo, draw up a lp, yo, draw through 2 lps on hook, yo, insert hook in same st, yo, draw up a lp, yo, draw through 2 lps on hook, yo, draw through all 3 lps on hook.

Beginning cluster (beg cl): Ch 2 *(counts as first dc)*, yo, insert hook in same st, yo, draw up lp, [yo, draw through 2 lps on hook] twice.

INSTRUCTIONS

SEAT COVER
Row 1: With size J hook and A, work **sc foundation st** *(see Foundation Stitches on page 172)* 23 times, turn. *(23 sc)*

Row 2: Ch 1, 2 sc in first sc, sc in each of next 21 sc, 2 sc in last sc, turn. *(25 sc)*

Row 3: Ch 1, sc in each sc across, turn.

Row 4: Ch 1, 2 sc in first sc, sc in each sc across to last sc, 2 sc in last sc, turn. *(27 sc)*

Row 5: Rep row 3.

Row 6: Rep row 4. *(29 sc)*

Rows 7–9: Rep row 3.

Row 10: Rep row 4. *(31 sc)*

Rows 11–14: Rep row 3.

Row 15: Rep row 4. *(33 sc)*

Rows 16–29: Rep row 3.

Row 30: Ch 1, sk first sc, sc across to last 2 sc, sk next sc, sc in last sc, turn. *(31 sc)*

Rows 31 & 32: Rep row 3.

Rows 33–46: [Rep rows 30 and 31 alternately] 7 times. *(17 sc at end of last row)*

Row 47: Ch 1, sk first 2 sc, sc in each of next 12 sc, sk next 2 sc, sc in last sc, turn. *(13 sc)*

Row 48: Ch 1, sk first sc, sc in next sc, sk next sc, sc in each of next 6 sc, sk next sc, sc in next sc, sk next sc, sc in last sc. Fasten off. *(9 sc)*

BORDER
Rnd 1 (RS): With size J hook, join A in first row end st in

bottom right corner, ch 1, sc in each of next 48 row end sts down length, sc in each of next 9 sc across top, sc in each of next 48 row end sts down length, 3 sc in first ch across bottom of foundation row, sc in each of next 21 chs, 3 sc in last ch, **join** (see Pattern Notes) in first sc. Fasten off.

Rnd 2: Join B in 2nd sc of 3-sc of right corner, **beg cl** (see Special Stitches) and dc in same st, **cl** (see Special Stitches) and dc in same 2nd sc of same 3-sc of corner, [cl in next sc, dc in next sc] around, working (cl, dc) twice in each center corner sc, join in top of beg cl. Fasten off.

Rnd 3: Working in **front lp only** (see Stitch Guide), join C in front lp of beg cl of previous rnd, ch 1, [sc in front lp of each of next 2 sts, (ch 3, sl st) in last sc made] around, join in beg sc.

Rnd 4: Working behind rnd 3 in **back lps** only (see Stitch Guide) of rnd 2, join B in back lp of beg cl, beg cl in same st, dc in back lp of next st, [cl in back lp of next st, dc in back lp of next st] around, join in beg cl.

Row 5: Now working in rows around 3 sides of Cover only, ch 1, sc in beg cl, [ch 1, sk next st, sc in next st] rep around 3 sides to within last 21 sts, do not work across bottom, turn.

Row 6: Ch 1, sc in first sc, sc in next ch-1 sp, [ch 1, sk next sc, sc in next ch-1 sp] across 3 sides to within last sc, sc in last sc, turn.

Row 7: Ch 1, sc in first sc, [ch 1, sk next sc, sc in next ch-1 sp] across 3 sides to within last 2 sc, ch 1, sk next sc, sc in last sc, turn.

Row 8: Rep row 6. Fasten off.

DRAWSTRING
With B, ch 195. Fasten off. Weave Drawstring through ch-1 sps of row 7.

SMALL YELLOW FLOWER
Make 11.
Rnd 1: With size J hook and B, ch 2, 7 sc in 2nd ch from hook, join in first sc. Fasten off.

Rnd 2: Join D in beg sc, ch 1, (sc, ch 4, sc) in each sc around, join in beg sc. Fasten off.

SMALL PINK FLOWER
Make 2.
Rnd 1: With size J hook and D, ch 2, 7 sc in 2nd ch from hook, join in first sc. Fasten off.

Rnd 2: Join B in beg sc, ch 1, (sc, ch 4, sc) in each sc around, join in beg sc. Fasten off.

LARGE ROSE
Make 1 single strand rose with size J hook and 2 double strand roses with size K hook.
Rnd 1: With B, make **slip ring** (see Foundation Stitches on page?), ch 1, [sc in ring, ch 3] 8 times, join in beg sc. (8 sc)

Rnd 2: Sl st in beg ch-3 sp, ch 1, (sc, hdc, dc, hdc, sc) in each ch-3 sp around, **do not join**.

Rnd 3: Working behind petals of rnd 2, [**bpsc** (see stitch guide) around post of next sc of rnd 1,

ch 4] 8 times, join in beg bpsc.

Rnd 4: Sl st in beg ch-4 sp, ch 1, (sc, hdc, 3 dc, hdc, sc) in each ch-4 sp around, join in beg sc. Fasten off.

LARGE LEAF
Make 2 single strand leaves with size J hook and 4 double strand leaves with size K hook.
Rnd 1: With C, work sc foundation st 8 times, ch 2, working on bottom of foundation row, sc in base of each sc across, ch 2, join in beg sc. (16 sc)

Rnd 2: Ch 3 (counts as first dc), dc in same sc as ch-3, hdc in each of next 2 sc, sc in each of next 3 sc, sl st in each of next 2 sc, (sl st, ch 3, sl st) in ch-2 sp, sl st in each of next 2 sc, sc in each of next 3 sc, hdc in each of next 2 sc, 2 dc in next sc, 8 tr in next ch-2 sp, join in 3rd ch of ch-3. Fasten off.

SEAT COVER ACCENTS
Sew 1 single strand Large Rose to center of Seat Cover and sew 1 Small Yellow Flower to center of Rose. Sew 1 single strand Leaf to each side of Rose on the left and right side. Sew 1 Small Yellow Flower to top center of Seat Cover. Sew 1 Small Yellow Flower to each bottom corner on the right and left side of Seat Cover.

RUG
Row 1: With size K hook and 2 strands of A held tog, work **sc foundation st** (see Foundation Stitches on page?) 45 times, turn. (45 sc)

Rows 2–73: Ch 1, sc in each sc across, turn. At the end of row 73, fasten off.

RUG BORDER

Rnd 1 (RS): Join 2 strands of B in top right corner sc, ch 3 *(counts as first dc)*, ***cl** (see Special Stitches)* in next sc, dc in next sc*, ◊rep from * to * across to next corner, ch 2 *(corner sp)*, cl in first row, dc in next row, cl in next row, dc in next row, **sk next row, [cl in next row end st, dc in next row] twice**, rep from ** to ** across to last 4 rows, sk next row, cl in next row, dc in each of next 2 rows, ch 2◊, dc in first ch across foundation row, rep from ◊ to ◊, **join** *(see Pattern Notes)* in 3rd ch of ch-3.

Rnd 2: Ch 3, cl in each cl and dc in each dc around, work (dc, ch 2, dc) in each corner ch-2 sp, join in 3rd ch of ch-3. Fasten off.

Rnd 3: Join 2 strands of C in top of beg ch-3 of previous rnd, ch 1, sc in each cl and sc in each dc around, working (sc, ch 2, sc) in each corner ch-2 sp, join in beg sc. Fasten off.

Rnd 4: Join 2 strands of B in beg sc of previous rnd, ch 3, *[cl in next sc, dc in next sc] across to within 1 sc from corner, cl in next sc, (2 dc, ch 2, 2 dc) in corner ch-2 sp, dc in next sc, rep from * around, cl in next sc, dc in next sc, join in 3rd ch of ch-3. Fasten off.

Rnd 5: Join 2 strands of C with sl st in beg sc of previous rnd, ch 1, sc in same st, (sc, ch 3, sl st) in next sc, [sc in next sc, (sc, ch 3, sl st) in next sc] around, counting each corner ch-2 sp as 2 sts, join in beg sc. Fasten off.

RUG ACCENTS

Sew 1 double strand Rose to center of each end of Rug approximately 12 rows in on winter white section. Sew 1 Small Yellow Flower to center of each Rose. Sew 1 double strand Leaf to left and right side of each Rose. Sew 1 Small Yellow Flower in each of the 4 outside corners where winter white meets light country rose.

BATHROOM TISSUE COVER

Rnd 1: With size J hook and A, make **slip ring** *(see Foundation Stitches on page ?)*, ch 3, 15 dc in slip ring, **join** *(see Pattern Notes)* in 3rd ch of ch-3. *(16 dc)*

Rnd 2: Ch 3 *(counts as first dc)*, dc in same st as beg ch-3, 2 dc in each dc around, join in 3rd ch of ch-3. *(32 dc)*

Rnd 3: Ch 3, 2 dc in next dc, [dc in next dc, 2 dc in next dc] around, join in 3rd ch of ch-3. *(48 dc)*

Rnd 4: Ch 1, sc in each dc around, join in beg sc.

Rnd 5: Ch 1, sc in each sc around, **do not join**, use st marker to mark rnds.

Rnds 6–20: Sc in each sc around. At the end of rnd 20, sl st in next sc. Fasten off.

Rnd 21: Join C in first sc of previous rnd, ch 1, sc in same sc, (sc, ch 3, sl st) in next sc, [sc in next sc, (sc, ch 3, sl st) in next sc] around, join in beg sc. Fasten off.

TOP FLORAL ACCENT

With size J hook and C, work sc foundation st, *insert hook in base ch just completed, yo, draw lp through, yo, draw through 1 lp on hook, yo, draw through 2 lps on hook*, (ch 3, sl st) in top of last sc, [rep from * to * twice, (ch 3, sl st) in top of last sc] 14 times, join in first sc. Fasten off. Sew to center top of Bathroom Tissue Cover.

CENTER FLOWER

Rnd 1: With B, make a slip ring, ch 1, [sc in ring, ch 3] 8 times, join in beg sc.

Rnd 2: Sl st in next ch-3 sp, ch 1, (sc, hdc, dc, hdc, sc) in each ch-3 sp around, join in beg sc. Fasten off.

Sew Center Flower centered on top of Bathroom Tissue Cover inside Top Floral Accent. Sew 1 Small Yellow Flower to center of light country rose flower. Sew 1 Small Pink Flower to center front and back of Bathroom Tissue Cover.

SMALL LEAF
Make 4.

With size J hook and C, ch 4, dc in first ch of ch-4, (ch 3, sl st) in top of last dc made, dc, hdc in same first ch of beg ch-4. Fasten off.

Sew 1 Leaf to each side of each Small Pink Flower. ●

Prissy Pup Pad

BY **BENDY CARTER**

SKILL LEVEL ◼◼◼◻
INTERMEDIATE

FINISHED SIZE
17 x 23 x 5½ inches

MATERIALS
- TLC Essentials medium (worsted) weight yarn (6 oz/312 yds/170g per skein): 6 skeins #2313 Aran
- Size H/8/5mm crochet hook or size needed to obtain gauge
- Tapestry needle
- Sewing needle
- Light pink sewing thread
- Light green sewing thread
- Straight pins
- Fiberfill
- Stitch marker
- 5 yds ¼-inch-wide ribbon: 1 each light pink and light green ribbon
- 60 inches round cord elastic
- Foam pad: 13½ wide x 19½ long x 2 inches thick
- 28-quart plastic box, inside top of box is 15 x 21 inches, inside bottom of box 14 x 20 inches, outside top of box 17 x 23 inches and 5½ inches tall

GAUGE
Sc/dc pattern: 12½ sts = 4 inches; 11½ rows = 4 inches

PATTERN NOTE
Weave in loose ends as work progresses.

INSTRUCTIONS

TOP MATTRESS COVER
Row 1 (RS): Work **sc foundation st** (see Foundation Stitches on page 172) 41 times, then work last st, yo, insert hook in base of last st (so that 2 lps are below hook), yo, draw through, yo, draw through 1 lp (creates base), yo, draw through 3 lps on hook (hdc st), turn. (42 sc)

Row 2: Ch 1, sc in first st, [dc in next st, sc in next st] across to last st, hdc in last st, turn. (42 sts)

Rep row 2 until Cover measures 19½ inches from beg. Fasten off.

FIRST BOTTOM MATTRESS COVER
Work First Bottom Mattress Cover same as Top Mattress Cover until Bottom is 4 rows less than Top Cover. Fasten off.

2ND BOTTOM MATTRESS COVER
Work 2nd Bottom Mattress Cover same as Top Mattress Cover until 8 rows are completed. Fasten off.

MATTRESS LONG SIDE
Make 2.
Rep row 1 of Top Mattress Cover for 5 sts then work last st of row 1, turn. (6 sts)

Rep row 2 of Top Mattress Cover until piece measures 19½ inches from beg. Fasten off.

MATTRESS SHORT SIDE
Make 2.
Rep the same as Mattress Long Side until piece measures 13½ inches from beg. Fasten off.

SEWING
With RS facing, whipstitch Long and Short Sides to Top Mattress Cover. In same way, sew the four corner seams of sides, creating a little basket; turn the basket RS out.

Place 2nd Bottom Mattress Cover down on table with RS facing down, place First Bottom Mattress Cover down on table with RS facing down, overlapping 2nd Bottom Mattress Cover by 4 rows. This overlapped section will be left open to insert foam pad mattress. Place basket, with Sides down on top of Bottom pieces, pin Sides to Bottom pieces with WS facing.

BOX LINING
Rnd 1 (RS): Join yarn with sl st in corner where Sides and Bottom are pinned, inserting hook through Side piece then through Bottom piece, ch 1, working through both thicknesses, sc evenly sp around,

working 58 sc sts across each long side, 39 sc across each short side and 3 sc in each corner, **do not join**, use place st marker to mark rnd. *(206 sc)*

Rnd 2: Working in **front lps** *(see Stitch Guide)* for this rnd only, sc in each st around.

Rnd 3: Sc in each st around.

Rep rnd 3 until Box Lining measures 2½ inches from beg.

Rnd 4: Sc around, inc 3 sc evenly sp on each side. *(218 sc)*

Rep rnd 3 until Box Lining measures 5 inches from beg.

Rnd 5: Rep rnd 4. *(230 sc)*

Rep rnd 3 until Box Lining measures 7½ inches from beg, mark last rnd to weave elastic cord through later, **do not fasten off**.

RUFFLE
Rnd 1 (RS): [Ch 3, sc in **back lp only** *(see Stitch Guide)* of next sc] around.

Rnd 2: [Ch 3, sc in next ch-3 lp] around.

Rep rnd 2 until Ruffle measures 4½ inches. Fasten off.

ASSEMBLY
Place foam pad inside Mattress Cover, place in bottom of plastic box with Box Lining going up and over sides of box.

Weave elastic cord in and out of sc sts of marked rnd. Pull elastic cord so that it creates a snug fit around top of box. Tie ends of elastic in a tight knot, trim and hide ends. Unused lps of rnd will help hide elastic. Ruffle should end about ¼ inch from bottom of box.

PILLOW
Note: *To dec in pat: leave sts to be decreased unworked. If next to last st to be worked on a row is a sc st, work hdc for the last st. If next to last st to be worked on row is a dc st, work sc for last st. Always beg a row with a sc st.*

FIRST HALF
Rep rows 1 and 2 of Top Mattress Cover.

For shaping, continue working in established pattern, at the same time, dec 1 st at end of next 8 rows, dec 2 sts at end of next 6 rows, dec 3 sts at end of next 2 rows, last row will have 16 sts. Fasten off.

2ND HALF
Turn First Half upside down, with RS facing, join yarn in base, working in base of sts, [rep row 2 of Top Mattress Cover] 3 times.

Rep First Half of shaping of pillow.

STUFFING & RUFFLE
Row 1 (RS): Fold Pillow piece in half with WS facing, join yarn at opening with sl st, ch 1, working through both thicknesses, sc evenly sp around opening until 3 inches rem open, stuff Pillow lightly with fiberfill, then sc across rem opening, turn.

Row 2: Ch 1, sc in first sc, [ch 3, sc in next sc] across, turn.

Row 3: Sl st in ch-3 sp, ch 1, (sc, ch 3, sc) in same ch sp, [(sc, ch 3, sc) in next ch-3 sp] across. Fasten off.

BED & PILLOW BOWS
Cut 18 light green ribbons and 17 light pink ribbons, each 10 inches long. Attach a light pink ribbon at elastic level on each corner of box then tie ribbons into bows. In like manner, alternating light green and light pink, attach 5 bows evenly across each short side of box and 7 bows evenly across each long side of box.

In like manner, starting with a light green, then alternating colors, attach 7 bows evenly sp on Pillow between Pillow and Ruffle.

Using matching sewing thread, sew bows securely in place. ●

Pathways Doily

BY **LORI ZELLER**

SKILL LEVEL ◼◼◼▢ INTERMEDIATE

FINISHED SIZE
11¾ x 15½ inches

MATERIALS
- Crochet cotton size 10:
    200 yds white
    80 yds each blue and navy
- Size 6/1.80mm steel crochet hook or size needed to obtain gauge
- Tapestry needle
- Knitting needle size 13
- Stitch marker

GAUGE
First motif = 1¼ x 2 inches; 4 dc = ⅜ inch; 9 dc rows = 2 inches

PATTERN NOTES
Weave in loose ends as work progresses.

Join with slip stitch as indicated unless otherwise stated.

Work a swatch of double crochet stitches before beginning for accurate gauge.

SPECIAL STITCH
Fan: (Dc, ch 1) twice and dc in st or sp indicated.

INSTRUCTIONS

DOILY CENTER
First Motif
Rnd 1: Wrap white, work **rolled ring foundation st** *(see Foundation Stitches on page 172)*, wrapping white around knitting needle 7 times, slip ring off knitting needle, work 20 sc over ring, draw up a lp, remove hook and place lp on knitting needle and wind white around knitting needle 6 more times, slip ring off knitting needle and work 20 sc in ring, **join** *(see Pattern Notes)* in first sc on 2nd ring.

Rnd 2: Sl st in next sc, ch 1, sc in same sc, [ch 3, sk next sc, sc in next sc] 8 times, ch 3, sc in 2nd sc of first ring, [ch 3, sk next sc, sc in next sc] 8 times, ch 2, join in first sc.

Rnd 3: Sl st in first ch-3 sp, ch 1, sc in same sp, [ch 3, sc in next ch-3 sp] 4 times, place st marker in last ch-3 sp made, ch 3, [sc in next ch-3 sp, ch 3] around, join in first sc. Fasten off.

2nd Motif
Rnds 1 & 2: Rep rnds 1 and 2 of First Motif.

Rnd 3: Sl st in first ch-3 sp, ch 1, sc in same sp, [ch 3, sc in next ch-3 sp] 3 times, ch 1, sl st in marked ch-3 sp on First Motif, ch 1, sc in next ch-3 sp on 2nd Motif *(motifs are now joined into a strip)*, ch 3, [sc in next ch-3 sp, ch 3] around, join in first sc, **do not fasten off**.

Rnd 4: Sl st in first ch-3 sp, ch 1, sc in same sp, [ch 3, sc in next ch-3 sp] twice, ch 1, sc in first unworked sp on next motif, [ch 3, sc in next ch-3 sp] 16 times, ch 1, sc in first unworked sp on next motif, [ch 3, sc in next ch-3 sp] 13 times, ch 3, join in first sc.

Rnd 5: Sl st in first ch-3 sp, ch 1, sc in same sp, *dc eyelet 3 times *(see Foundation Stitches on page ?)*, sk next 3 ch sps, sc in next ch sp, [dc eyelet twice, sk next ch-3 sp, sc in next ch-3 sp] twice, [dc eyelet twice, sc in next ch-3 sp] 5 times, [dc eyelet twice, sk next ch-3 sp, sc in next ch-3 sp] twice, rep from * around, dc eyelet twice, join in first sc.

Rnd 6: Sl st under ch-3 sp of first dc eyelet, ch 1, sc in same sp, ch 4, 2 dc in 4th ch from hook, place marker in first dc of last 2-dc group, [sc in ch-3 sp of next eyelet, ch 4, 2 dc in 4th ch from hook] around, join in first sc. Fasten off.

Rnd 7: Join blue with sc around marked dc, ch 4, [sc around dc under next ch-4, ch 4] around, join in first sc.

Rnd 8: Sl st in first ch-4 sp, ch 1, sc in same sp, [ch 4, sc in next ch-4 sp] 7 times, *ch 4, sc in same sp, [ch 4, sc in next ch-4 sp] twice, ch 4, sc in same sp, [ch 4, sc in next ch-4 sp] 3 times, ch 4, sc in same sp, [ch 4, sc in next ch-4 sp] twice, ch 4, sc in same sp*, [ch 4, sc in next ch-4 sp] 14 times, rep from * to *, [ch 4, sc in next ch-4 sp] 6 times, ch 4, join in first sc.

Rnd 9: Sl st in first ch-4 sp, ch 1, sc in same sp, [ch 4, sc in next ch-4 sp] 7 times, place marker in last ch-4 sp made, ch 4, [sc in next ch-4 sp, ch 4] around, join in first sc. Fasten off blue.

Rnd 10: Join navy with sc in marked ch-4 sp, *[ch 4, sc in next ch-4 sp] twice, ch 4, sc in same sp*, rep from * to *, [ch 4, sc in next ch-4 sp] 3 times, ch 4, sc in same sp, rep from * to *, [ch 4, sc in next ch-4 sp] 18 times, ch 4, sc in same sp, rep from * to *, [ch 4, sc in next ch-4 sp] 3 times, ch 4, sc in same sp, rep from * to *, ch 4, [sc in next ch-4 sp, ch 4] around, join in first sc.

Rnd 11: Sl st in first ch-4 sp, ch 1, sc in same sp, [ch 4, sc in next ch-4 sp] 7 times, ch 4, sc in same sp, [ch 4, sc in next ch-4 sp] 29 times, ch 4, sc in same sp, ch 4, [sc in next ch-4 sp, ch 4] around, join in first sc. Fasten off.

Rnd 12: Join white with sc in first ch-4 sp of previous rnd, ch 1, **fan** *(see Special Stitch)* in next ch-4 sp, ch 1, [sc in next ch-4 sp, ch 1, fan in next ch-4 sp, ch 1] around, join in first sc.

Rnd 13: Sl st in first ch-1 sp, ch 1, sc in same sp, dc eyelet twice, sc in ch-1 sp after fan, dc eyelet, [sc in next ch-1 sp, dc eyelet twice, sc in ch-1 sp after fan, dc eyelet] around, join in first sc.

Rnd 14: Sl st under ch-3 sp of first dc eyelet, ch 1, sc in same sp, ch 5, sc in ch-3 sp of next eyelet, [ch 5, sk next dc eyelet, sc in ch-3 sp of next eyelet, ch 5, sc in ch-3 sp of next eyelet] around, ch 2, dc in first sc to join.

Rnd 15: Ch 1, sc in same sp as joining, ch 5, [sc in next ch-5 sp, ch 5] around, join in first sc. Fasten off.

Rnd 16: Join blue with sc in first ch-5 sp on previous rnd, dc eyelet twice, sc in next ch-5 sp, dc eyelet, working in front of previous rnd, sc under ch-3 of sk dc eyelet on rnd 13, dc eyelet, *sc in next ch-5 sp on previous rnd, dc eyelet twice, sc in next ch-5 sp, dc eyelet, working in front of previous rnd, sc under ch-3 of sk dc eyelet on rnd 13, dc eyelet, rep from * around, join in first sc. Fasten off.

Rnd 17: Join navy with sc under ch-3 sp of first dc eyelet, ch 5, dc under ch-3 of next eyelet, [ch 5, sk next 2 dc eyelets, sc under ch-3 sp of next eyelet, ch 5, dc under ch-3 of next eyelet] around, ch 2, dc in first sc to join.

Rnd 18: Ch 1, sc in same sp as joining, ch 5, [sc in next ch-5 sp, ch 5] around, join in first sc. Fasten off.

BRUGES LACE BAND

Row 1: With white, ch 5, yo, insert hook in 5th ch from

hook, yo, draw lp through, yo, draw through 1 lp on hook *(base ch completed)*, [yo, draw through 2 lps on hook] twice, *yo insert hook in last base ch completed, yo, draw lp through, yo, draw through 1 lp on hook *(base ch)*, [yo, draw through 2 lps on hook] twice, rep from * twice, *(4 dc and 1 beg ch-5 sp)*, ch 2, sc in first ch-5 sp on rnd 18, turn.

Row 2: Ch 2, dc in each dc, turn.

Row 3: Ch 5, dc in each dc, ch 2, sc in next ch-5 sp on rnd 18, turn.

Rows 4–12: [Rep rows 2 and 3 alternately] 5 times, ending with row 2.

Row 13: Ch 5, dc in each dc, ch 2, sc in same ch-5 sp on rnd 18 as before, turn.

Rows 14–24: [Rep rows 2 and 3 alternately] 6 times, ending with row 2.

Row 25: Rep row 13.

Rows 26–30: [Rep rows 2 and 3 alternately] 3 times, ending with row 2.

Row 31: Rep row 13.

Rows 32–74: [Rep rows 2 and 3 alternately] 22 times, ending with row 2.

Row 75: Rep row 13.

Rows 76–80: [Rep rows 2 and 3 alternately] 3 times, ending with row 2.

Row 81: Rep row 13.

Rows 82–92: [Rep rows 2 and 3 alternately] 6 times, ending with row 2.

Row 93: Rep row 13.

Rows 94–98: [Rep rows 2 and 3 alternately] 3 times, ending with row 2.

Row 99: Rep row 13.

Rows 100–135: [Rep rows 2 and 3 alternately] 18 times.

Row 136: Ch 2, dc in each dc. Leaving a 6-inch length, fasten off.

Sew top of dc sts of row 136 to corresponding base chs on row 1.

OUTER SECTION
Rnd 1: Join navy with sc in first ch-5 sp on Bruges Lace Band, [ch 5, sc in next ch-5 sp] around, ch 2, dc in first sc to join.

Rnd 2: Ch 1, sc in same sp as joining, dc eyelet twice, [sc in next ch-5 sp, dc eyelet twice] around, join in first sc. Fasten off.

Rnd 3: Make a slip knot on hook with blue, insert hook under ch-3 sp pf last dc eyelet made, yo, draw lp through, insert hook under ch-3 sp of next dc eyelet, yo, draw lp through, yo, draw through all lps on hook, dc eyelet twice, *[insert hook under ch-3 sp of next dc eyelet, yo, draw lp through] twice, yo, draw through all lps on hook, dc eyelet twice, rep from * around,

join in first sc. Fasten off blue.

Rnd 4: Join white with sc in first dc eyelet made on previous rnd, ch 5, sc in next 2 dc eyelets, *ch 5, sc in next 2 dc eyelets, rep from * until 1 eyelet rem, ch 5, sc in last eyelet, join in first sc.

Rnd 5: Ch 1, sc in same st as joining, (sc, ch 4, sc) in next ch-5 sp, [sc in each of next 2 sc, (sc, ch 4, sc) in next ch-5 sp] around until 1 sc rem, sc in last sc, join in first sc.

Rnd 6: Sl st in next sc, sl st in next ch-4 sp, ch 1, (sc, dc eyelet, sc) in same ch-4 sp, dc eyelet, [(sc, dc eyelet, sc) in next ch-4 sp, dc eyelet] around, join in first sc.

Rnd 7: Sl st under ch-3 sp of first dc eyelet, ch 1, sc in same sp, ch 3, [sc in next ch-3 sp, ch 3] around, join in first sc.

Rnd 8: Sl st in first ch-3 sp, ch 1, sc in same sp, [ch 3, sc in next ch-3 sp] 7 times, *ch 3, sc in same ch-3 sp as last sc, [ch 3, sc in next ch-3 sp] 3 times*, rep from * to * 7 times, ch 3, sc in same ch-3 sp as last sc, [ch 3, sc in next ch-3 sp] 42 times, rep from * to * 8 times, ch 3, sc in same ch-3 sp as last sc, [sc in next ch-3 sp, ch 3] around, join in first sc.

Rnds 9–12: Sl st in first ch-3 sp, ch 1, sc in same sp, ch 3, [sc in next ch-3 sp, ch 3] around, join in first sc.

Rnd 13: Sl st in first ch-3 sp, ch 1, sc in same sp, dc eyelet, [sc in next ch-3 sp, dc eyelet] around, join in first sc. Fasten off. ●

Blue Shells Doily

BY **KATHERINE ENG**

SKILL LEVEL
INTERMEDIATE

FINISHED SIZE
10¾ inches in diameter

MATERIALS
- DMC Traditions size 10 crochet cotton (350 yds per ball):
    1 ball #5798 delft blue
- Size 5/1.90mm steel crochet hook or size needed to obtain gauge

GAUGE
Rnds 1–4, point to point = 2 inches

PATTERN NOTES
Weave in loose ends as work progresses.

Join with slip stitch as indicated unless otherwise stated.

SPECIAL STITCHES
Shell: (3 dc, ch 2, 3 dc) in indicated st or sp.

V-stitch (V-st): (Dc, ch 1, dc) in indicated st or sp.

INSTRUCTIONS

DOILY
Rnd 1: Work **rolled ring** (see Foundation Stitches on page 172), 12 sc in ring, **join** (see Pattern Notes) in first sc. (12 sc)

Rnd 2: Ch 1, sc in first sc, [ch 3, sc in next sc] around, hdc in beg sc to form last ch sp. (12 sc, 12 ch-3 sps)

Rnd 3: Ch 1, sc in same sp as beg ch-1, [ch 3, sc in next ch-3 sp] around, hdc in beg sc to form last ch sp.

Rnd 4: Ch 1, sc in same sp as beg ch-1, **shell** (see Special Stitches) in next ch sp, [sc in next ch sp, shell in next ch sp] around, join in beg sc. (6 shells, 6 sc)

Rnd 5: Ch 4 (counts as first dc, ch-1), dc in same sc, *ch 1, shell in next ch-2 sp, ch 1**, **V-st** (see Special Stitches) in next sc, rep from * around, ending last rep at **, join in 3rd ch of beg ch-4. (6 shells, 6 V-sts)

Rnd 6: Sl st in next ch-1 sp, ch 4, dc in next ch-1 sp, *ch 1, shell in next ch-2 sp, [ch 1, dc in next ch-1 sp] 3 times, rep from * around, ch 1, dc in next ch-1 sp, ch 1, join in 3rd ch of beg ch-4. (6 shells, 18 dc)

Rnd 7: Sl st in next ch-1 sp, ch 4, dc in next ch-1 sp, *ch 1, shell in next ch-2 sp**, [ch 1, dc in next ch-1 sp] 4 times, rep from * around, ending last rep at **, [ch 1, dc in next ch-1 sp] twice, ch 1, join in 3rd ch of beg ch-4.

Rnd 8: Ch 1, sc in each dc and each st around, working (sc, ch 2, sc) in each ch-2 sp, join in first sc, **turn**.

Rnd 9 (WS): Ch 1, sc in each sc around, working (sc, ch 2, sc) in each ch-2 sp, join in beg sc, **turn**.

Rnd 10 (RS): (Ch 3, 2 dc, ch 2, 3 dc) in same sc, *[ch 1, sk 1 sc, dc in next sc] 4 times, ch 1, sk next sc, shell in next ch-2 sp, [ch 1, sk 1 sc, dc in next sc] 4 times**, ch 1, sk next sc, shell in next sc, rep from * around, ending last rep at **, sc in top of beg ch-3 to form last ch-1 sp, sl st in same sp.

Rnd 11: Ch 4, *shell in next ch-2 sp**, [ch 1, dc in next ch-1 sp] 5 times, ch 1, rep from * around, ending last rep at **, [ch 1, dc in next ch-1 sp] 4 times, ch 1, join in 3rd ch of ch-4, sl st in next ch-1 sp.

Rnd 12: Ch 4, *shell in next ch-2 sp**, [ch 1, dc in next ch-1 sp] 6 times, ch 1, rep from * around, ending last rep at **, [ch 1, dc in next ch-1 sp] 5 times, join in 3rd ch of ch-4, sl st in next ch-1 sp.

Rnd 13: Ch 4, *shell in next ch-2 sp, ch 1, dc in each of next

3 ch-1 sps, (tr, ch 3, tr) in next ch-1 sp**, dc in each of next 3 ch-1 sps, ch 1, rep from * around, ending last rep at **, dc in each of next 2 ch-1 sps, join in 3rd ch of ch-4.

Rnd 14: Ch 1, sc in same ch as joining, *sk next 4 sts, shell in next ch-2 sp, sk next 3 dc, sk next ch-1 sp, sc in next dc, sk next 3 sts, shell in next ch-3 sp, sk next 3 sts**, sc in next dc, rep from * around, ending last rep at **, join in beg sc.

Rnd 15: Ch 3, shell in next ch-2 sp, dc in next sc, shell in next ch-2 sp, *dc in next sc, dc in each of next 3 dc, (2 dc, tr, ch 2, tr, 2 dc) in next ch-2 sp, dc in each of next 3 dc**, [dc in next sc, shell in next ch-2 sp] 3 times, rep from * around, ending last rep at **, dc in next sc, shell in next ch-2 sp, join in 3rd ch of beg ch-3. *(6 large points, 18 shells)*

Rnd 16: Ch 1, sc in each st around, working (sc, ch 2, sc) in each ch-2 sp around, join in first sc, **turn**.

Rnd 17 (WS): Rep rnd 9.

Rnd 18: Ch 1, sc in next sc, *ch 2, sk next 2 sc, sc in next sc, rep from * around working at each shell point, ch 2, sk 2 sc, (sc, ch 3, sc) in ch-2 sp and at each large point, ch 2, sk 2 sc, (sc, ch 2, sc, ch 4, sc, ch 2, sc) in ch-2 sp, join in first sc. Fasten off.

With WS facing, block lightly. ●

Woven Basket

BY **ELLEN GORMLEY**

SKILL LEVEL

FINISHED SIZE
7½ x 10 inches in diameter

MATERIALS
- Red Heart Super Saver medium (worsted) weight yarn (7 oz/364 yds/198g per skein):
    1 skein #256 carrot
    3 oz #316 soft white
- TLC Essentials medium (worsted) weight yarn (7 oz/364 yds/198g per skein):
    3 oz each #2335 taupe and #2112 black
- Size I/9/5.5mm crochet hook or size needed to obtain gauge
- Yarn needle
- 24 stitch markers

GAUGE
7 sc rnds = 2 inches in diameter; 7 sc = 2 inches

PATTERN NOTES
Weave in loose ends as work progresses.

Join with slip stitch as indicated unless otherwise stated.

INSTRUCTIONS

BOTTOM
Rnd 1 (RS): Starting at center with carrot, work **slip ring**

foundation st (*see Foundation Stitches on page 172*) 6 times in ring, do not join, use st marker and move marker as work progresses. (*6 sc*)

Rnd 2: 2 sc in each sc around. (*12 sc*)

Rnd 3: [Sc in next sc, 2 sc in next sc] 6 times. (*18 sc*)

Rnd 4: [Sc in each of next 2 sc, 2 sc in next sc] 6 times. (*24 sc*)

Rnd 5: [Sc in each of next 3 sc, 2 sc in next sc] 6 times. (*30 sc*)

Rnd 6: [Sc in each of next 4 sc, 2 sc in next sc] 6 times. (*36 sc*)

Rnd 7: [Sc in each of next 5 sc, 2 sc in next sc] 6 times. (*42 sc*)

Rnd 8: [Sc in each of next 6 sc, 2 sc in next sc] 6 times. (*48 sc*)

Rnd 9: [Sc in each of next 7 sc, 2 sc in next sc] 6 times. (*54 sc*)

Rnd 10: [Sc in each of next 8 sc, 2 sc in next sc] 6 times. (*60 sc*)

Rnd 11: [Sc in each of next 9 sc, 2 sc in next sc] 6 times. (*66 sc*)

Rnd 12: [Sc in each of next 10 sc, 2 sc in next sc] 6 times. (*72 sc*)

Rnd 13: [Sc in each of next 11 sc, 2 sc in next sc] 6 times. (*78 sc*)

Rnd 14: [Sc in each of next 12 sc, 2 sc in next sc] 6 times. (*84 sc*)

Rnd 15: [Sc in each of next 13 sc, 2 sc in next sc] 6 times. (*90 sc*)

Rnd 16: [Sc in each of next 14 sc, 2 sc in next sc] 6 times, sl st in next st. Fasten off. (*96 sc*)

VERTICAL STRIPS
Note: *Place a stitch marker in every 4th st of rnd 16 of Bottom. When working verticals, 1 sc between each vertical will rem unworked.*

Row 1: Join carrot with sc in first marked st, sc in each of next 2 sc, turn. (*3 sc*)

Row 2: Ch 1, sc in each of next 3 sc, turn.

Rows 3–20: Rep row 2. At the end of row 20, fasten off.

[Rep rows 1–20 consecutively] 23 times. At the end of last rep, **do not fasten off**.

TOP
Rnd 1: Ch 1, sc in first sc, sc in each of next 2 sc, ch 1, [working across next Vertical Strip, sc in each of next 3 sc, ch 1] 23

times, **join** *(see Pattern Notes)* in beg sc. *(72 sc, 24 ch-1 sps)*

Rnd 2: Ch 2 *(counts as first hdc)*, hdc in next 2 sc, sc in next ch-1 sp, [hdc in each of next 3 sc, hdc in next ch-1 sp] 23 times, join in beg sc. *(96 sc)*

Rnd 3: [Ch 1, sl st in next hdc] around. Fasten off.

HORIZONTAL STRIPS
Make 3 each taupe, black and white.
Note: *Various colors may differ in size and gauge. Make 1 strip each color and compare. Horizontal Strips measure 26 inches.*

Row 1: Work **sc foundation st** *(see Foundation Stitches page?)* 75 times, turn. *(75 sc)*

Row 2: Ch 1, sc in each sc across. Leaving an 8-inch length, fasten off.

WEAVE
[Weave white, taupe, then black Horizontal Strips through Vertical Strips] 3 times, sewing beg and end of each Horizontal Strip tog as work progresses. ●

Pacific Place Setting

BY **DIANE SIMPSON**

SKILL LEVEL ■■□□
EASY

FINISHED SIZES
Place Mat: 13½ x 19½ inches

Napkin Ring: 2½ inches wide x 2½ inches in diameter

MATERIALS
- Lily Sugar 'n Cream Stripes medium (worsted) weight yarn (2 oz/95 yds/56g per ball): 2 balls #21143 country stripes   **4** **MEDIUM**
- Size K/10½/6.5mm crochet hook or size needed to obtain gauge
- Yarn needle

GAUGE
7 sc = 2½ inches; 6 sc rows = 2 inches

PATTERN NOTES
Weave in loose ends as work progresses.

Join with slip stitch as indicated unless otherwise stated.

INSTRUCTIONS

PLACE MAT
Row 1: Starting at short edge, work **sc foundation st** *(see Foundation Stitches on page 172)* 37 times, turn. *(37 sc)*

Row 2: Ch 1, sc in each st across, turn.

Rows 3–13: Rep row 2.

Row 14: Ch 2 *(counts as first hdc)*, hdc in next st, [ch 1, sk next st, hdc in next st] 17 times, hdc in last st, turn. *(20 hdc, 17 ch-1 sps)*

Row 15: Ch 1, sc in first hdc, [ch 1, sk next hdc, sc in next ch-1 sp] 17 times, ch 1, sk next hdc, sc in next hdc, turn. *(19 sc, 18 ch-1 sps)*

Row 16: Ch 2, hdc in next ch-1 sp, [ch 1, sk next sc, hdc in next ch-1 sp] 17 times, hdc in last sc, turn. *(20 hdc, 17 ch-1 sps)*

Rows 17–21: Rep row 2. *(37 sc)*

Rows 22–45: [Rep rows 14–21 consecutively] 3 times.

Rows 46–53: Rep row 2. At the end of row 53, **do not fasten off.**

BORDER
Rnd 1: Ch 1, sc in each st across, ch 1 at corner, sc in end of same row, sc in each row across edge, ch 1 at corner, sc in base of each st across foundation row, ch 1 at corner, sc in end of same row, sc in each row across edge, ch 1, **join** *(see Pattern Notes)* in first sc. *(180 sc, 4 ch-1 sps)*

Rnd 2: Ch 1, **reverse sc** *(see Fig. 1 on page 107)* in each sc and each ch-1 sp around, join in first sc. Fasten off. *(184 sts)*

NAPKIN RING
Rnd 1: Work **sc foundation st** *(see Foundation Stitches on page 172)* 16 times, join in first sc. *(16 sc)*

Rnd 2: Ch 3 *(counts as first hdc, ch-1)*, sk next sc, [hdc in next sc, ch 1, sk next sc] 7 times, join in 2nd ch of beg ch-3. *(8 hdc, 8 ch-1 sps)*

Rnd 3: Ch 1, sc in first st, sc in next ch-1 sp, [ch 1, sk next hdc, sc in next ch-1 sp] 7 times, join in first sc. *(9 sc, 7 ch-1 sps)*

CONTINUED ON PAGE 107

Salt & Pepper Place Mat

BY **KATHLEEN STUART**

SKILL LEVEL ■■□□
EASY

FINISHED SIZE
12 x 17 inches

MATERIALS
- Lion Cotton medium (worsted) weight yarn (solid: 5 oz/236 yds/140g; multi-colors: 4 oz/ 189 yds/113g per ball):
   2 balls #201 salt and pepper
   1 ball #112 poppy red
- Size G/6/4mm crochet hook or size needed to obtain gauge
- Yarn needle

GAUGE
Shell, V-st, shell = 2¼ inches; 4 rows = 2¼ inches

PATTERN NOTES
Weave in loose ends as work progresses.

Join with slip stitch as indicated unless otherwise stated.

SPECIAL STITCHES
Shell: 3 dc in indicated st.

V-stitch (V-st): (Dc, ch 1, dc) in indicated st.

INSTRUCTIONS

PLACE MAT
Row 1: Starting at short edge, work **small V-st foundation** *(see Foundation Stitches on page 172)*, *yo 3 times, insert hook in same ch as last V-st was worked in, yo, draw lp through, [yo, draw through 2 lps on hook] twice *(2 chs completed)*, yo, draw through 1 lp on hook *(base ch completed)*, [yo, draw through 2 lps on hook] twice, **yo, insert hook in last base ch completed, yo, draw lp through, [yo, draw through 2 lps on hook] twice, rep from ** once more *(shell completed with 3 dc)*, yo 3 times, insert hook in same ch last shell was worked in, yo, draw lp through, [yo, draw through 2 lps on hook] twice *(2 chs completed)*, yo, draw through 1 lp on hook *(base ch completed)*, [yo, draw through 2 lps on hook] twice, ch 1, yo, insert hook in last base ch completed, yo, draw lp through [yo, draw through 2 lps on hook] twice *(V-st completed)*, rep from * until 20 V-sts and 20 shell sts *(or desired width of Place Mat ending with shell)*, yo 2 times, insert hook in last base ch completed, yo, draw lp through, yo, draw through 2 lps on hook *(1 ch completed)*, yo, draw through 1 lp on hook *(base ch completed)*, [yo, draw through 2 lps on hook] twice *(last dc completed)*.

Row 2: Ch 3 *(counts as first dc)*, *sk 2 sts, **shell** *(see Special Stitches)* in center dc of 3-dc group, **V-st** *(see Special Stitches)* in ch-1 sp of V-st, rep from * across, dc in last dc, turn.

Row 3: Ch 3, *V-st in ch-1 sp of V-st, shell in center dc of 3-dc group, rep from * across, dc in last dc, turn.

Rows 4–19: [Rep rows 2 and 3 alternately] 8 times.

Row 20: Rep row 2.

Rnd 21: Now working in rnds, ch 1, 3 sc in first st *(for corner)*, sc in each st and each ch-1 sp across with 3 sc in corner st, sc evenly sp across ends of rows, 3 sc in corner st, sc in each st across opposite side of

foundation row, 3 sc in corner st, sc evenly sp across ends of rows, **join** *(see Pattern Notes)* in first sc.

Rnd 22: Ch 2 *(counts as first hdc)*, working in **back lps only** *(see Stitch Guide)*, hdc in each st around, working 3 hdc in each center corner st, join in 2nd ch of beg ch. Fasten off.

Rnd 23: Working in rem **front lps** *(see Stitch Guide)* of rnd 21, join poppy red with sl st in any st, **reverse sc** *(see Fig.1)* in each st around, join in first sc. Fasten off. ●

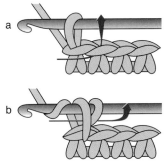

Fig. 1
Reverse Single Crochet

Vertical Shells Table Runner

BY **MARTY MILLER**

SKILL LEVEL ■■■□ INTERMEDIATE

FINISHED SIZE
10½ x 40 inches

MATERIALS
- J&P Coats Royale Gemini Double Strand size 3 crochet cotton (300 yds per ball): 2 balls #445 frosty green/oasis
- Size N/15/10mm crochet hook or size needed to obtain gauge
- Yarn needle

4 MEDIUM

GAUGE
[Shell, ch 3] twice = 2 inches; 5 shell rows = 2 inches

PATTERN NOTE
Weave in loose ends as work progresses.

SPECIAL STITCH
Shell: 3 dc in indicated st.

INSTRUCTIONS

RUNNER
Foundation row: Ch 4, 3 dc in first ch of ch-4, yo hook twice,

CONTINUED ON PAGE 108

Flower Basket Wall Hanging

BY **LUCILLE LAFLAMME**

SKILL LEVEL
■■■□ INTERMEDIATE

FINISHED SIZE
32 x 44 inches

MATERIALS
· J&P Coats Royale Fashion Crochet size 3 crochet cotton (150 yds per ball):
    10 balls #926 bridal white
· Size C/2/2.75mm crochet hook or size needed to obtain gauge

GAUGE
7 dc = 1 inch; 3 dc rows = 1 inch

PATTERN NOTES
Weave in loose ends as work progresses.

Join with slip stitch as indicated unless otherwise stated.

At the end of each round, fasten off yarn, join next color in following color sequence: [A, B, C, D, E, F, G, H] 4 times.

SPECIAL STITCHES
Lacet with picot: Ch 3, sk next 2 sts, (sc in next st, ch 3, sl st in top of last sc), ch 3, sk next 2 sts, dc in next st; on following row,

ch 5 above Lacet with picot.

Picot: Ch 3, sl st in top of last st.

INSTRUCTIONS

WALL HANGING

Row 1: Ch 5, beg in first ch of ch-5, work **dc, ch 1 foundation** *(see Foundation Stitches on page 172)* 74 times, turn. *(74 ch sps)*

Row 2: Ch 3 *(counts as first dc)*, [2 dc in next ch sp, dc in next dc] twice, *[ch 2, dc in next dc] 6 times, [2 dc in next ch sp] twice, rep from * across, turn.

Row 3: Ch 3, dc in each of next 6 dc, *[ch 2, dc in next dc] 6 times, dc in each of next 6 dc, rep from * across, turn.

Row 4: Ch 5 *(counts as first dc, ch 2)*, sk next 2 sts, dc in next st, ch 2, sk next 2 sts, dc in next st, 2 dc in next sp, dc in next dc *(block)*, [ch 2, sk next 2 sts, dc in next dc] 4 times *(4 sps)*, 2 dc in next ch sp, dc in next dc *(block)*, [ch 2, sk next 2 dc, dc in next dc] twice *(2 sps)*, *2 dc in next sp, dc in next dc *(block)*, [ch 2, sk next 2 sts, dc in next dc] 4 times *(4 sps)*, 2 dc in next ch sp, dc in next dc, [ch 2, sk next 2 dc, dc in next dc] twice, rep from * across, turn.

Rows 5–112: Ch 5, using sts of row 4 as a guide for blocks and sps, follow chart for rows 5–112. At the end of row 112, **do not turn**.

EDGING

Rnd 1: Ch 6 *(counts as first tr, ch 2)*, tr in same corner st, (ch 2, tr) 5 times in same corner st, *[ch 5, sk next 3 rows, 3 sc in next row, ch 5, sk next 3 rows, tr in next row, (ch 2, tr) 4 times in same row] 13 times across edge, ch 5, sk next 3 rows, 3 sc in next row, ch 5, tr in corner st, (ch 2, tr) 6 times in same st, [ch 5, sk next 3 sps, 3 sc in next sp, ch 5, sk next 3 sps, tr in next sp (ch 2, tr) 4 times in same sp] 8 times across end, ch 5, sk 4 sps, 3 sc in next sp, ch 5**, tr in corner st, (ch 2,

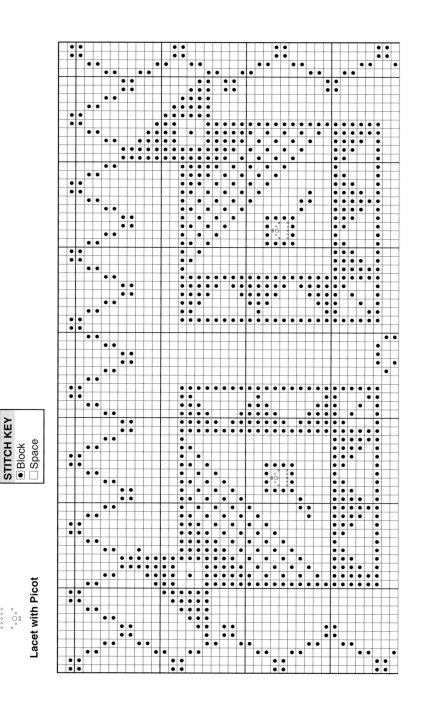

STITCH KEY
● Block
☐ Space

Lacet with Picot

tr) 6 times in same corner st, rep from * around, ending last rep at **, **join** (see Pattern Notes) in 4th ch of ch-6.

Rnd 2: Ch 1, *sc in first tr of corner, ch 3, dc in next tr, **picot** (see Special Stitches), ch 3, sc in next tr, ch 3, (dc, picot) 3 times in next tr, ch 3, sc in next tr, ch 3, dc, picot in next tr, ch 3, sc in next tr, [5 sc in ch-5 sp, sc in next sc, ch 2, (dc, picot, dc) in next sc, ch 2, sc in next sc, 5 sc in ch-5 sp, sc in next tr, ch 3, (dc, picot) in next tr, ch 2, (dc, picot, dc) in center tr, ch 2, (dc, picot) in next tr, ch 3, sc in next tr] rep across edge, rep from * around outer edge, join in first sc. Fasten off. ●

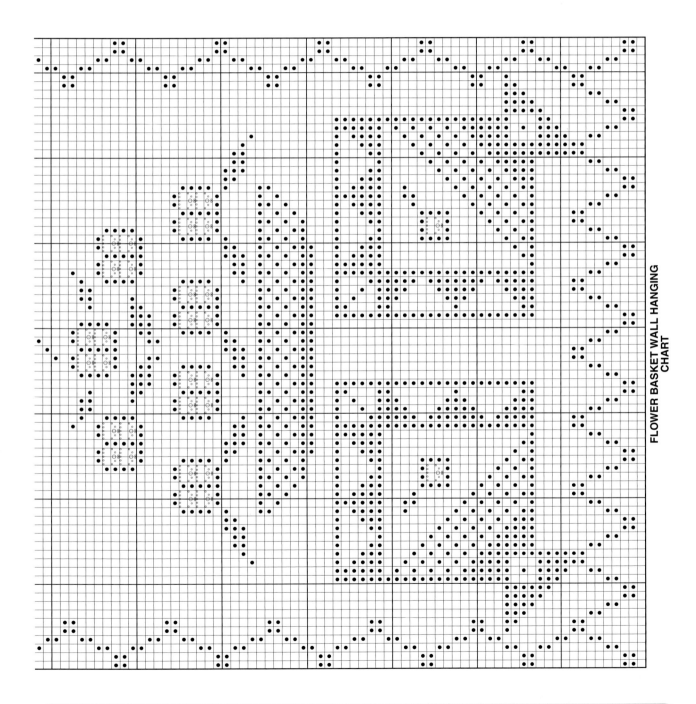

FLOWER BASKET WALL HANGING CHART

Penguin Rug

BY **KATHLEEN STUART**

SKILL LEVEL ■□□ EASY

FINISHED SIZE
27 inches, including Feet

MATERIALS
- Caron Perfect Match medium (worsted) weight yarn (7 oz/355 yds/198g per skein):
   1 skein #7776 orange
- Red Heart Super Saver medium (worsted) weight yarn (7 oz/364 yds/198g per skein):
   1 skein each #311 white and #312 black
- Size N/15/10mm crochet hook or size needed to obtain gauge
- Yarn needle

GAUGE
6 dc = 3½ inches;
1 dc rnd = 1 inch

PATTERN NOTES
Weave in loose ends as work progresses.

Join with slip stitch as indicated unless otherwise stated.

Wind each skein into 4 equal balls of yarn.

Rug is crocheted with 4 strands of yarn held together throughout.

INSTRUCTIONS

BODY
Rnd 1 (RS): Starting at center **with 4 strands white held tog** (*see Pattern Notes*), work **dc foundation st** (*see Foundation Stitches on page 172*) 3 times in same st (*4 dc*), work 14 dc foundation sts, work 7 more dc foundation sts in same st as last dc (*8 dc in same st*), working on opposite side, dc in each of next 13 sts, 4 dc in same base st as beg ch, **join** (*see Pattern Notes*) in 3rd ch of beg ch, **do not turn rnds**. (*42 dc*)

Rnd 2: Ch 1, 2 sc in same st as beg ch-1, 2 sc in each of next 2 sts, sc in each of next 5 sts, hdc in next st, dc in each of next 9 sts, 2 dc in each of next 6 sts, dc in each of next 9 sts, hdc in next st, sc in each of next 5 sts, 2 sc in each of next 3 sts, join in first sc. (*54 sts*)

Rnd 3: Ch 1, 2 sc in same st as beg ch-1, sc in next st, [2 sc in next st, sc in next st] twice, sc in each of next 6 sts, hdc in next st, dc in each of next 8 sts, [2 dc in next st, dc in next st] 6 times, sc in each of next 8 sts, hdc in next st, sc in each of next 6 sts, [2 sc in next st, sc in next st] 3 times, join in first sc. (*66 sts*)

Rnd 4: Ch 2 (*counts as first hdc*), hdc in same st as beg ch, hdc in each of next 2 sts, [2 hdc in next st, hdc in each of next 2 sts] twice, hdc in each of next 5 sts, sc in next st, hdc in next st, dc in each of next 8 sts, [2 dc in next st, dc in each of next 2 sts] 6 times, dc in each of next 8 sts, hdc in next st, sc in next st, hdc in each of next 5 sts, [2 hdc in next st, hdc in each of next 2 sts] 3 times, join in 2nd ch of ch-2. (*78 sts*)

Rnd 5: Ch 3 (*counts as first dc*), dc in each of next 2 sts, 2 dc in next st, [dc in each of next 3 sts, 2 dc in next st] twice, dc in each of next 4 sts, hdc in next st, sc in next st, hdc in next st, dc in each of next 8 sts, [dc in each of next 3 sts, 2 dc in next st] 6 times, dc in each of next 8 sts, hdc in next st, sc in next st, hdc in next st, dc in each of next 4 sts, [dc in each of next 3 sts, 2 dc in next st] 3 times, join in 3rd ch of beg ch, **change color** (*see Stitch Guide*) to 4 strands of black. Fasten off white. (*90 sts*)

Rnd 6: Ch 3, dc in same st, dc in each of next 4 sts, [2 dc in next st, dc in each of next 4 sts] twice, dc in each of next 4 sts, hdc in next st, sc in next st, hdc in next st, dc in each of next 8 sts, [2 dc in next st, dc in each of next 4

sts] 6 times, dc in each of next 8 sts, hdc in next st, sc in next st, hdc in next st, dc in each of next 4 sts, [2 dc in next st, dc in each of next 4 sts] 3 times, join in 3rd ch of beg ch. *(102 sts)*

Rnd 7: Ch 3, dc in each of next 4 sts, 2 dc in next st, [dc in each of next 5 sts, 2 dc in next st] twice, dc in each of next 4 sts, hdc in next st, sc in next st, hdc in next st, dc in each of next 8 sts, [dc in

each of next 5 sts, 2 dc in next st] 6 times, dc in each of next 8 sts, hdc in next st, sc in next st, hdc in next st, dc in each of next 4 sts, [dc in each of next 5 sts, 2 dc in next st] 3 times, join in 3rd ch of beg ch. *(114 sts)*

Rnd 8: Ch 3, dc in each of next 24 sts, hdc in next st, sc in next st, hdc in next st, dc in each of next 8 sts, [2 dc in next st, dc in each of next 6 sts] 6 times, dc in

each of next 8 sts, hdc in next st, sc in next st, hdc in next st, dc in each of next 25 sts, join in 3rd ch of beg ch. Fasten off. *(120 sts)*

FEET
Make 2.
Row 1: With 4 strands of orange held tog and WS of Rug facing, join orange with sc in 70th *(58th for 2nd foot)* st of rnd

CONTINUED ON PAGE 108

Ripple Afghan

BY **RAYNELDA CALDERON**

SKILL LEVEL ◼◼◻◻
EASY

FINISHED SIZE
32 x 51 inches

MATERIALS
- Lion Brand Vanna's Choice medium (worsted) weight yarn (solid: 3½ oz/170 yds/100g; print: 3 oz/145 yds/85g per ball):
    14 balls #202 purple print
    1 ball #147 purple
- Size J/10/6mm crochet hook or size needed to obtain gauge
- Yarn needle

GAUGE
10 bpsc = 4 inches; 15 rows = 5¼ inches

PATTERN NOTES
Weave in loose ends as work progresses.

Join with slip stitch as indicated unless otherwise stated.

INSTRUCTIONS

AFGHAN
Foundation row: Starting at bottom edge, work **hdc foundation st** *(see Foundation Stitches on page 172)* 152 times, turn.

CONTINUED ON PAGE 109

Misty Moonlight Pillow

BY **KATHERINE ENG**

SKILL LEVEL ◼️◼️◻️◻️
EASY

FINISHED SIZE
Fits 14-inch pillow

MATERIALS
- Plymouth Encore Colorspun Chunky (chunky) weight yarn (3½ oz/143 yds/100g per ball):
   2 balls #7127 teal/ purple multi
- Size I/9/5.50mm crochet hook or size needed to obtain gauge
- Tapestry needle
- Heavy sewing thread
- 14-inch matching pillow
- 2 matching 1½-inch buttons

6 SUPER BULKY

GAUGE
4 eyelets across = 5 inches;
Rows 1–3 = 1½ inches

PATTERN NOTES
Weave in loose ends as work progresses.

Join with slip stitch as indicated unless otherwise stated.

Finished piece measures 13½ inches square and will stretch to fit pillow.

CONTINUED ON PAGE 109

Dishcloth Duo

BY **DIANE SIMPSON**

ROUND DISHCLOTH

SKILL LEVEL ■■□□
EASY

FINISHED SIZE
10 inches in diameter

MATERIALS
- Lily Sugar 'n Cream Twists medium (worsted) weight yarn (2 oz/95 yds/56g per ball):
  1 ball #20010 natural twists
- Size I/9/5.5mm crochet hook or size needed to obtain gauge

GAUGE
Rnd 1 = 1¾ inches

PATTERN NOTES
Weave in loose ends as work progresses.

Join with slip stitch as indicated unless otherwise stated.

SPECIAL STITCHES
Single crochet shell (sc shell): (Sc, ch 1, sc) in indicated st or sp.

Shell: (2 dc, ch 1, 2 dc) in indicated st or sp.

Beginning half shell (beg half shell): Ch 3, dc in same st as joining.

Ending half shell: 2 dc in same st as beg ch-3, sc in 3rd ch of beg ch-3.

Picot: Ch 3, sc in 3rd ch from hook.

INSTRUCTIONS

DISHCLOTH
Rnd 1: Starting at center, form **slip ring** (see Foundation Stitches on page 172), ch 4 (counts as first dc, ch 1), (dc, ch 1) 7 times in slip ring, **join** (see Pattern Notes) with sc in 3rd ch of beg ch-4. (8 dc, 8 ch-1 sps)

Rnd 2: Ch 1, **sc shell** (see Special Stitches) in same sp as beg ch-1, ch 1, [sc shell in next ch-1 sp, ch 1] around, join in first sc. (8 sc shells)

Rnd 3: Beg half shell (see Special Stitches), ch 1, [**shell** (see Special Stitches) in next ch-1 sp of sc shell, ch 1] around, **ending half shell** (see Special Stitches). (8 shells, 8 ch-1 sps)

Rnd 4: Ch 1, sc shell in joining, ch 1, [sc shell in next ch-1 sp, ch 1] 15 times, join in first sc. (16 sc shells, 16 ch-1 sps)

Rnd 5: Beg half shell, ch 1, dc in next ch-1 sp of sc shell, ch 1, [shell in next ch-1 sp of next sc shell, ch 1, dc in next ch-1 sp of next sc shell, ch 1] around, ending half shell. (8 shells, 8 dc, 16 ch-1 sps)

Rnd 6: Rep rnd 4. (24 sc shells, 24 ch-1 sps)

Rnd 7: Beg half shell, ch 1, *[dc in next ch-1 sp of sc shell, ch 1] twice**, shell in ch-1 sp of next sc shell, ch 1, rep from * around, ending last rep at **, ending half shell. (8 shells, 16 dc, 24 ch-1 sps)

Rnd 8: Rep rnd 4. (32 sc shells, 32 ch-1 sps)

Rnd 9: Beg half shell, dc in next ch-1 sp of sc shell, [shell in next ch-1 sp of sc shell, dc in next ch-1 sp of sc shell] around, ending half shell. (16 shells, 16 dc)

Rnd 10: Ch 1, (sc, **picot**—see Special Stitches, sc) in same st, ch 1, *(sc, picot, sc) in single dc between shells, ch 1**, (sc, picot, sc) in next ch-1 sp of shell, ch 1, rep from * around, ending last rep at **, join in first sc. Fasten off. (32 picots, 64 sc, 32 ch-1 sps)

Weave in loose end.

CONTINUED ON PAGE 110

Felted Barstool Pad

BY **BENDY CARTER**

SKILL LEVEL
INTERMEDIATE

FINISHED SIZE
Fits Barstool with 12½-inch seat.

Measure across top of seat and including thickness of seat, total measurement should not exceed 15 inches.

MATERIALS
- Moda Dea Bamboo Wool medium (worsted) weight yarn (2¾ oz/145 yds/80g per ball):
  3 balls #3365 coffee
  1 ball each #3620 celery, #3920 chili pepper and #3650 bamboo
- Size H/8/5mm crochet hook or size needed to obtain gauge
- Tapestry needle
- Straight pins
- 12 inches diameter x 1-inch thick foam pad
- 40 inches ¹⁄₁₆-inch cord elastic
- 2 white drawstring stoppers
- 14-inch diameter piece of cardboard

GAUGE
14 sts = 4 inches; 16 rows = 4 inches

PATTERN NOTES
Weave in loose ends as work progresses.

Join with slip stitch as indicated unless otherwise stated.

INSTRUCTIONS

TRIANGLES
Make 12 each coffee and bamboo and 13 chili pepper.
Row 1 (WS): Leaving a long tail for sewing, work **sc foundation st** (see Foundation Stitches on page 172) 17 times, turn. (17 sc)

Row 2 (RS): Ch 1, **sc dec** (see Stitch Guide) in next 2 sc, sc in each rem sc across, turn. (16 sc)

Row 3: Rep row 2, **change color** (see Stitch Guide) to celery in last st. (15 sc)

Row 4: Rep row 2. (14 sc)

Row 5: Rep row 2, changing back to Triangle color in last st. Fasten off celery. (13 sc)

Rows 6–16: Rep row 2. (2 sc)

Row 17: Ch 1, sc dec in next 2 sc. Leaving a long length for sewing, fasten off. (1 sc)

SEWING & FELTING
Place Triangles tog side by side according to chart. Sew the 37 triangles together, using mattress stitch joining. Find center of center Triangle. From center point, piece should measure 10½ inches or larger in every direction so that a 21-inch circles could be created.

Felt pieces in hot water until it has shrunk by ⅓. Piece should now be the correct size to create a 14-inch circle. All stitches should have disappeared. Let piece dry completely then, using cardboard as guide, cut piece into a 14-inch circle.

EDGING
Row 1: Leaving a long tail for sewing, using coffee, ch 2, insert hook in 2nd ch from hook, yo, draw through, yo, draw through 1 lp on hook (creates base), yo, draw through both lps on hook, [insert hook in base of last st (so that 2 lps are below hook), yo, draw through, yo, draw through 1 lp on hook (creates base), yo, draw through both lps on hook] 7 times, ch 1, insert hook in base of last st, yo, draw through, [yo, draw through 1 lp on hook] 2 times (creates ch-1 and base for next st), yo, draw through both lps on hook, insert hook in base of last st, yo, draw through, yo, draw through 1 lp on hook, yo, draw through both lps on hook, turn. (10 sts)

Row 2: Ch 1, sc, ch 1, sk ch-1 sp, sc in next st across, turn.

Row 3: Ch 1, sc in each of next 8 sts, ch 1, sk ch-1 sp, sc in next st, turn.

Rep rows 2 and 3 alternately until Edging measures 60 inches. Leaving a length long enough to sew to Edging to seat, fasten off.

SEWING & FELTING
Place Edging piece and Seat piece side by side so that ch-1 sps on Edging are farthest from

CONTINUED ON PAGE 111

Colonial Foundation Afghan

BY **LISA PFLUG**

SKILL LEVEL ◼◻◻ EASY

FINISHED SIZE
47 x 59 inches, excluding Fringe

MATERIALS

- Lion Brand Vanna's Choice medium (worsted) weight yarn (3½ oz/170 yds/100g per ball): 6 balls each #130 honey (A), #133 brick (B) and #105 silver blue (C)
- Size J/10/6mm crochet hook or size needed to obtain gauge
- Yarn needle
- 5 stitch markers

GAUGE
11 dc = 4⅛ inches; 4 rows = 2 inches

PATTERN NOTES
Weave in loose ends as work progresses.

Join with slip stitch as indicated unless otherwise stated.

INSTRUCTIONS

SQUARE 1
Make 8.
Row 1: With A, work **sc** **foundation st** (see Foundation Stitches on page 172) 30 times, turn. (30 sc)

Row 2: Ch 1, sc in each sc across, turn.

Row 3: Rep row 2.

Row 4 (RS): Ch 3 (counts as first tr), tr in each sc across, turn.

Rows 5–7: Rep row 2.

Row 8: Rep row 4.

Rows 9–20: [Rep rows 5–8 consecutively] 3 times.

Rows 21–23: Rep row 2. At the end of row 23, fasten off.

SQUARE 2
Make 7.
Row 1 (foundation row): With B, work **hdc foundation st** (see Foundation Stitches on page 172) 30 times, turn. (30 hdc)

Row 2: Ch 1, hdc in each hdc across, turn.

Rows 3–22: Rep row 2. At the end of row 22, fasten off.

ASSEMBLY
Using B, whipstitch 5 squares tog to form 2 strips of (A, B, A, B, A) with tr sts of Square 1 blocks on RS.

Using B, whipstitch 5 squares tog to form 1 strip of (B, A, B, A, B) with tr sts of Square 1 blocks on RS.

STRIP EDGING
Note: When changing colors, leave a 26-inch length of yarn at beg or end to use for stitching.

Rnd 1: Changing A and B colors as needed to match Squares, attach yarn to upper left corner of strip with RS facing, ch 1, sc in same corner, *work [ch 1, sc] 93 times evenly sp along row ends up to next corner, ch 1, (sc, ch 1, sc) in corner, ch 1, work 30 sc across to next corner, (sc, ch 1, sc) in corner, rep from * around, ch 1, **join** (see Pattern Notes) in beg sc. Fasten off.

RECTANGLE
Make 2.
Row 1 (foundation row): With C, work **dc foundation st** (see Foundation Stitches on page 172) 15 times, turn. (15 dc)

Row 2: Ch 2, dc in each dc across, turn.

Row 3: Ch 1, sc in first st, sc in each of next 2 sts, [**fptr** *(see Stitch Guide)* in corresponding dc 2 rows below, sk st directly behind fptr, sc in next st] 5 times, sc in each of next 2 sts, turn.

Row 4: Rep row 2.

Row 5: Ch 1, sc in first sc, sc in each of next 2 sts, [fptr in fptr directly below, sk st directly behind fptr, sc in next st] 5 times, sc in each of next 2 sts, turn.

Rows 6–59: [Rep rows 4 and 5 alternately] 27 times. At the end of row 59, turn to work along left side with RS facing.

RECTANGLE EDGING
Rnd 1: Ch 1, sc in same corner st, *work [ch 1, sc] 93 times evenly sp along row ends to next corner, ch 1, (sc, ch 1, sc) in corner st, ch 1, work 15 sc across short edge, ch 1, (sc, ch 1, sc) in corner st, rep from * around, ch 1, join in first sc. Fasten off.

AFGHAN ASSEMBLY
With RS facing, use either A or B as appropriate to whipstitch strips and rectangles tog.

BORDER
Rnd 1: Join B in upper left corner of Afghan, ch 1, *sc in each sc and each ch-1 sp up to next corner, (sc, ch 1, sc) in corner ch-1 sp, sc in each sc to next corner*, (sc, ch 1, sc) in corner ch-1 sp, rep from * to * once, (sc, ch 1) in last corner, join in first sc to complete corner.

Rnd 2: Ch 1, *sc in each sc to next corner, (sc, ch 1, sc) in corner ch-1 sp, rep from * around, sc, ch 1 in same sc as first sc, join in first sc. Fasten off.

STAR CENTER
Make 7.
Rnd 1 (RS): For center, with C, ch 4, sl st in first ch to form a ring, ch 1, 10 sc in ring, join in first sc. *(10 sc)*

Rnd 2: Ch 1, 2 sc in each sc around, join in first sc. *(20 sc)*

Mark in every 4th sc of rnd 2

(5 sts marked with st markers).

STAR POINTS
Row 1 (RS): Join C to marked sc, ch 1, sc in same sc, sc in each of next 3 sc, turn. *(4 sc)*

Row 2: Ch 1, sc in each of next 4 sc, turn.

Row 3: Ch 1, sk first sc, sc in each of next 3 sc, turn. *(3 sc)*

Row 4: Ch 1, sc in each of next 3 sc, turn.

Row 5: Ch 1, sk first sc, sc in each of next 2 sc, turn. *(2 sc)*

Row 6: Ch 1, sc dec in next 2 sc. Fasten off. *(1 sc)*

Rep for all marked sts to form 5 Star Points, leaving 30-inch length on last point for sewing. Use tails to sew Stars onto front center of each Square 2.

FRINGE
Cut 14-inch lengths of A. Use 2 strands for each knot of fringe. Tie 1 knot around every other sc along short ends of Afghan. ●

Idaho Country Bed Spread CONTINUED FROM PAGE 72

BORDER
Rnd 1: With RS facing, **join** *(see Pattern Notes)* cotton in any corner, ch 4 *(counts as first dc, ch-1)*, [dc in next row, ch 1] around, working [dc, ch 1] 4 times in each corner, join in 3rd ch of beg ch-4.

Rnd 2: Ch 4, [dc in next dc, ch 1] around, working (dc, ch 2, dc) in center ch-1 sp of each corner, join in 3rd ch of beg ch-4.

Rnd 3: Sl st in next ch-1 sp, ch 3, [**fpdc** *(see Stitch Guide)* around next dc, dc in next ch-1 sp] around, working (dc, ch 2, dc) in each corner sp, join in 3rd ch of beg ch-3.

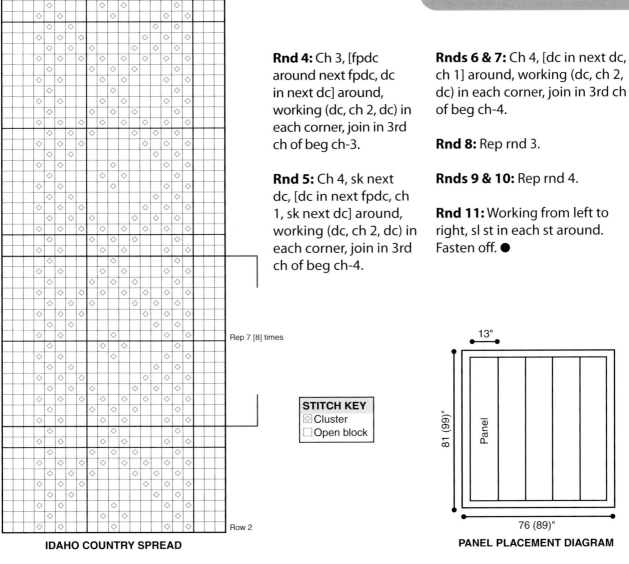

Rep 7 [8] times

STITCH KEY
◇ Cluster
□ Open block

Row 2

IDAHO COUNTRY SPREAD

Rnd 4: Ch 3, [fpdc around next fpdc, dc in next dc] around, working (dc, ch 2, dc) in each corner, join in 3rd ch of beg ch-3.

Rnd 5: Ch 4, sk next dc, [dc in next fpdc, ch 1, sk next dc] around, working (dc, ch 2, dc) in each corner, join in 3rd ch of beg ch-4.

Rnds 6 & 7: Ch 4, [dc in next dc, ch 1] around, working (dc, ch 2, dc) in each corner, join in 3rd ch of beg ch-4.

Rnd 8: Rep rnd 3.

Rnds 9 & 10: Rep rnd 4.

Rnd 11: Working from left to right, sl st in each st around. Fasten off. ●

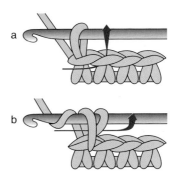

13"

81 (99)"

Panel

76 (89)"

PANEL PLACEMENT DIAGRAM

Pacific Place Setting CONTINUED FROM PAGE 88

Rnd 4: Ch 3, sk next st, [hdc in next ch-1 sp, ch 1, sk next sc] 7 times, join in 2nd ch of beg ch-3. *(8 hdc, 8 ch-1 sps)*

Rnd 5: Ch 1, sc in each hdc and each ch-1 sp around, join in beg sc, *(16 sc)*

Rnd 6: Ch 1, **reverse sc** *(see Fig. 1)* in each sc around, join in first sc. Fasten off.

Rnd 7: Join yarn in first ch of foundation rnd 1, ch 1, reverse sc in each st around, join in first sc. Fasten off. ●

a

b

**Fig. 1
Reverse Single Crochet**

Vertical Shells Table Runner CONTINUED FROM PAGE 92

insert hook in same first ch, yo, draw lp through, [yo, draw

through 2 lps on hook] twice *(2 foundation chs made)*, yo, draw through 1 lp *(base ch made)*, yo, draw through 2 lps on hook *(sc foundation st made)*, *ch 3, yo hook 4 times, insert hook in last base ch made, yo, draw up a lp, [yo, draw through 2 lps on hook] 3 times *(3 foundation chs made)*, yo, draw through 1 lp on hook *(base ch made)*, [yo, draw through 2 lps on hook] twice *(foundation dc made)*, 2 dc in last base ch made, yo hook twice, insert hook into same base ch, yo, draw up a lp, [yo,

draw through 2 lps on hook] twice *(2 foundation chs made)*, yo, draw through 1 lp *(base ch made)*, yo, draw through 2 lps *(foundation sc made)*, rep from * 9 more times, turn. *(11 shells)*

Row 1: Ch 3, **shell** *(see Special Stitch)* in first sc, sc in next ch-3 sp, ch 3, shell in next sc, [sc in next ch-3 sp, ch 3, shell in next sc] across, sc in last st, turn. *(11 shells)*

Rows 2–119: Rep row 1. At the end of row 119, fasten off. ●

Penguin Rug CONTINUED FROM PAGE 97

8 of Rug, sc in each of next 3 sts, turn. *(4 sc)*

Row 2: Ch 1, sc in first sc, ch 3, hdc in 2nd ch from hook, hdc in 3rd ch from hook, sc in next sc of row 1, ch 4, hdc in 2nd ch from hook, hdc in each of next 2 chs, sc in next sc of row 1, ch 3, hdc in 2nd ch from hook, hdc in next ch, (sc, sl st) in last sc of

row 1. Fasten off.

EYES
Rnd 1: With 4 strands of black, ch 2, 6 sc in 2nd ch from hook, join in first sc. Leaving an 8-inch length of yarn, fasten off.

Sew Eyes to Body between rnds 2–4, just to the side of the beg/end of those rnds, leaving a 1-inch sp between Eyes.

BEAK
Row 1: With 4 strands of orange, **sc foundation st** *(see Foundation Stitches page 172)* 3 times, turn. *(3 sc)*

Row 2: Ch 1, sk first st, sc in each of next 2 sts, turn. *(2 sc)*

Row 3: Ch 1, **sc dec** *(see Stitch Guide)* in next 2 sc. Fasten off. *(1 sc)*

Row 4: Working on opposite side of foundation sts, join 4 strands of orange with sc in first st, sc in each of next 2 sts, turn. *(3 sc)*

Row 5: Rep row 2.

Row 6: Rep row 3, **do not fasten off**.

Rnd 7: Now working in rnds, ch 1, sc evenly sp down side to row 3, (sc, ch 2, sc) in rem sc of row 3, sc evenly sp down opposite edge of Beak, work (sc, ch 2, sc) in last sc of row 6, join in first sc, leaving a 10-inch length of yarn. Fasten off.

Leaving rows 1–3 of Beak unsewn, sew rows 4–6 of Beak centered below Eyes over rnd 1 of Rug. ●

Ripple Afghan CONTINUED FROM PAGE 98

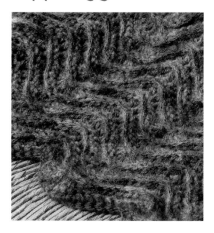

Row 1: Ch 2 *(counts as first dc)*, 4 dc in first hdc, *dc in next hdc, [sk next hdc, dc in next hdc] 8 times**, 5 dc in each of next 2 hdc, rep from * across, ending last rep at **, 5 dc in last hdc, turn. *(152 dc)*

Row 2: Ch 1, sc in first dc, **bpsc** *(see Stitch Guide)* in each dc across to last st, sc in last st, turn.

Row 3: Ch 2, 4 dc in first sc, *dc in next bpsc, [sk next bpsc, dc in next bpsc] 8 times**, 5 dc in each of next 2 bpsc, rep from * across, ending last rep at **, 5 dc in last st, turn.

Rep rows 2 and 3 alternately until piece measures approximately 51 inches, ending with row 3, draw up lp of purple. Fasten off purple print, **do not turn.**

BORDER
Rnd 1: Ch 1, working in ends of rows, [work 184 sc evenly sp across long edge, ch 1, sc in same st as last sc, work 152 sc across short edge, ch 1, sc in same st as last sc] twice, **join** *(see Pattern Notes)* in beg sc. Fasten off. ●

Misty Moonlight Pillow CONTINUED FROM PAGE 99

INSTRUCTIONS

PILLOW
Make 2.
Row 1: Working from bottom to top, **dc eyelet** *(see Foundation Stitches on page 172)* 9 times, turn. *(9 dc)*

Row 2: Ch 1, working back over dc sts, 2 sc over post of each dc and sc in each ch between dc sts across, turn. *(27 sc)*

Row 3: Ch 1, (sc, ch 2, sc) in first sc, [sk next sc, (sc, ch 2, sc) in next sc] across, turn.

Rows 4–27: Ch 1, (sc, ch 2, sc) in each ch-2 sp across, turn.

BORDER
Rnd 1: Working across top, (sc, ch 2, sc) in first ch-2 sp, work 2 sc in each of next 12 ch-2 sps, (2 sc, ch 2, sc) in last ch-2 sp *(27 sc)*; working across side, sc in end of each row to bottom working (sc, ch 2, sc) in end st *(27 sc)*; working across bottom, 2 sc over each ch 3 of beg and 1 sc in each st between chs working (sc, ch 2, sc) in last st *(27 sc)*, sc in end of each row to top joining last sc to first. Fasten off.

At end of 2nd piece, do not fasten off. With WS of pieces tog, work rnd 2 through both thicknesses.

Note: *Work pattern around 3 sides. Insert pillow and then complete.*

Rnd 2: (Sl st, ch 4, sl st) in corner ch-2 sp, [ch 2, sk 1 sc, sl st in next sc] around, working at each corner, ch 2, sk 1 sc, (sl st, ch 4, sl st) in corner sp, **join** *(see Pattern Notes)* in beg sl st. Fasten off.

With heavy thread, sew tog center of pillow and then attach a button at each side. ●

Dishcloth Duo CONTINUED FROM PAGE 100

SQUARE DISHCLOTH

SKILL LEVEL ◖■◻◻
EASY

FINISHED SIZE
9¾ x 10¾ inches

MATERIALS
• Lily Sugar 'n Cream
  Twists (worsted)
  weight yarn (2 oz/95
  yds/56g per ball):
    1 ball #20009 taupe twists

• Size I/9/5.5mm crochet hook
  or size needed to obtain
  gauge

GAUGE
Hdc in next st, [ch 1, sk next
st, hdc in next st] 6 times =
4 inches; [hdc row, sc row] 5
times = 4 inches

PATTERN NOTES
Weave in loose ends as work
progresses.

Join with slip stitch as indicated
unless otherwise stated.

INSTRUCTIONS

DISHCLOTH
Row 1: Starting at cuff, work
hdc foundation st *(see Foundation Stitches on page 172)*, [ch
1, hdc foundation st] 12 times,
hdc foundation st, turn. *(15 hdc,
12 ch-1 sps)*

Row 2: Ch 1, sc in first st, [ch 1,
sk next hdc, sc in next ch-1 sp]
across, sc in last st, turn.

Row 3: Ch 2 *(counts as first hdc)*,
hdc in next ch, [ch 1, sk next sc,
hdc in next ch] across, hdc in
last st, turn.

Rows 4–19: [Rep rows 2 and 3
alternately] 8 times.

Rnd 20: Now working in rnds,
ch 1, sc in each st and each ch
around, ch 1 at each corner, **join**
(see Pattern Notes) in beg sc.

Rnd 21: Ch 1, sc in each st
around, working (sc, ch 1, sc)
in each corner ch-1 sp, join in
beg sc.

Rnd 22: Ch 3 *(counts as first dc)*,
2 dc in same st, [sk next 2 sts, (sl
st, ch 3, 2 dc) in next st] around,
sk 1 st instead of 2 at corners, sl
st in same st as beg ch-3. Fasten
off. ●

Felted Barstool Pad CONTINUED FROM PAGE 103

Seat, pin Edging evenly sp around Seat. Using mattress st join, sew Edging to Seat.

Weave elastic cord in and out of ch-1 sps on Edging. Place a drawstring stopper on each end of elastic cord to hold in place.

Felt piece in hot water until edging has shrunk by ⅓, sts have disappeared and Edging piece and Seat piece have become one. Triangle circle should still measure 14 inches and Edging should measure 2 inches. Remove as much water as possible. Edging should fit snugly around barstool seat. If barstool is waterproof, place foam on barstool seat then place Barstool Pad on barstool seat to shape. If barstool is not waterproof, use another object same size as barstool seat to shape piece. Pull elastic to adjust fit around barstool seat. Barstool Pad will need to be removed from barstool seat in order for it to dry completely. Maintain barstool seat shape as much as possible when removing pad. ●

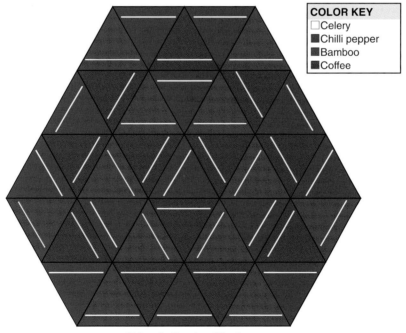

COLOR KEY
☐ Celery
■ Chilli pepper
■ Bamboo
■ Coffee

Triangle Sewing Chart

Wee Crochet

Chapter Contents

Pocket Bibs

BY ELLEN GORMLEY

BLUE BIB

SKILL LEVEL ◖■☐☐
EASY

FINISHED SIZE
10¼ x 11 inches, folded

MATERIALS
- Lion Brand Cotton-Ease medium (worsted) weight yarn (3½ oz/207 yds/100g per ball):
    1 ball each #110 lake, #186 maize and #100 snow
- Size I/9/5.5mm crochet hook or size needed to obtain gauge
- Yarn needle
- Straight pins

GAUGE
4 sc = 1 inch; 4 sc rows = 1 inch

PATTERN NOTES
Weave in loose ends as work progresses.

Join rounds with slip stitch unless otherwise stated.

INSTRUCTIONS

BIB
Row 1: Starting at neckline edge with lake, work **sc foundation st** (*see Foundation Stitches on page 172*) 17 times, turn. (*17 sc*)

Row 2: Ch 1, 2 sc in first sc, sc in each st across to last st, 2 sc in last st, turn. *(19 sc)*

Row 3: Ch 1, sc in each st across, turn.

Row 4: Rep row 3.

Rows 5–25: [Rep rows 2–4 consecutively] 7 times. *(33 sc)*

Row 26: Rep row 2. *(35 sc)*

Rows 27–55: Rep row 3. At the end of row 55, fasten off lake. **Do not turn**.

Row 56 (RS): Attach maize in first sc of previous row, ch 1, sc in same st as beg ch-1, sc in each st across, fasten off.

Row 57 (RS): Attach snow in first sc of previous row, ch 1, sc in same st as beg ch-1, sc in each sc across, fasten off.

Fold rows 48–57 upward and secure with straight pins.

EDGING

Row 1 (RS): Attach Maize in right bottom corner with sl st, ch 1, working through both thicknesses, work 8 sc up folded edge, sc in side edge of each row to row 1, *[work sc foundation st] 49 times *(first tie)*, ch 1, working in opposite side of foundation, sc in each of next 49 sts*, sc in opposite side of foundation across neckline, rep from * to * for 2nd tie, sc evenly sp down opposite edge of Bib to folded section, working through both thicknesses, work 8 sc across

edge. Fasten off. Remove straight pins.

Row 2 (RS): Attach snow with sl st in first sc of row 1 of Edging, ch 1, sc in same st as beg ch-1, sc in each st up side edge of Bib, sc across first tie, working 3 sc in ch-1 sp at end of tie, sc across opposite edge of tie, around neckline, sc around 2nd tie with 3 sc in end ch-1 sp and down opposite edge of Bib. Fasten off.

LIME BIB

SKILL LEVEL
EASY

FINISHED SIZE
10 x 12 inches

MATERIALS

- Lion Brand Cotton-Ease medium (worsted) weight yarn (3½ oz/207 yds/100g per ball):
    1 ball each #194 lime and #100 snow
- Size I/9/5.5mm crochet hook or size needed to obtain gauge
- Yarn needle
- Straight pins

GAUGE
[Sc, shell] 3 times = 4½ inches; 10 rows = 4½ inches

PATTERN NOTES
Weave in loose ends as work progresses.

CONTINUED ON PAGE 141

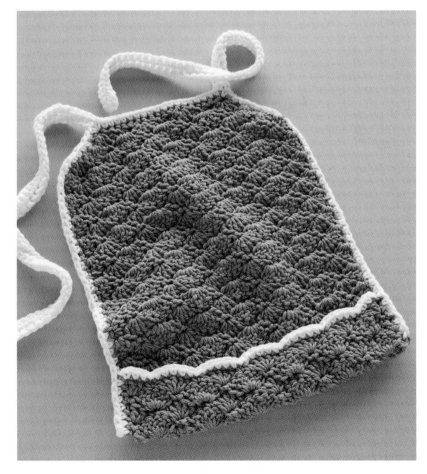

Precious in Pink

BY **LAURA GEBHARDT**

SKILL LEVEL ◼◼◻◻
EASY

FINISHED SIZES
Instructions given fit infant's size 6 months; changes for infant's size 12 months, 18 months and 24 months are in [ ]. When only 1 number is given, it applies to all sizes.

FINISHED GARMENT MEASUREMENTS
Chest: 19 inches *(6 months)* [20½ inches *(12 months)*, 22¼ inches *(18 months)* and 24 inches *(24 months)*]

MATERIALS
- Patons Beehive Baby Sport light (light worsted) weight yarn (solid: 3½ oz/359 yds/100g; variegated: 3 oz/304 yds/85g per ball):
    - 1 [2, 2, 2] balls #09420 precious pink *(MC)*
    - 1 ball #10415 hush-a-bye variegated *(CC)*
- Size F/5/3.75mm crochet hook or size needed to obtain gauge
- Yarn needle
- 3 pink 12mm shank buttons

GAUGE
19 dc = 4 inches; 14 dc rows = 6 inches

PATTERN NOTE
Weave in loose ends as work progresses.

INSTRUCTIONS

BACK
Row 1: Starting at bottom edge with MC, work **dc foundation st** *(see Foundation Stitches on page 172)* 45 [49, 53, 57] times, turn. *(45 [49, 53, 57] dc)*

Row 2: Ch 3 *(counts as first dc)*, dc in **back lp** *(see Stitch Guide)* of next st, [dc in **front lp** *(see Stitch Guide)* of next st, dc in back lp of next st] across to last dc, dc in last dc, turn.

Rep row 2 until Back measures 10 [11, 12, 13¼] inches from row 1. Fasten off.

LEFT FRONT
Row 1: Starting at bottom edge with MC, work dc foundation st 33 [35, 37, 39] times, turn. *(33 [35, 37, 39] dc)*

Row 2: Rep row 2 of Back.

Rep row 2 of Back until Left Front measures 2 [2, 3, 3] inches, ending with a RS row, turn.

Row 3 (WS): Ch 2 *(counts as a dec st)*, rep row 2 of Back across, turn. *(32 [34, 36, 38] dc)*

Row 4: Rep row 2 of Back to last 2 sts, **dc dec** *(see Stitch Guide)* in next 2 dc *(neck edge)*, turn. *(31 [33, 35, 37] dc)*

Next rows: [Rep rows 3 and 4 alternately] until 16 [18, 19, 22] rows are completed. Fasten off. *(15 [15, 16, 15] dc at end of last row)*

RIGHT FRONT
Row 1: Rep row 1 of Left Front.

Row 2: Rep row 2 of Back.

Rep row 2 of Back until Right Front measures 2 [2, 3, 3] inches, ending with a RS row, turn.

Row 3 (WS): Rep row 4 of Left Front. *(32 [34, 36, 38] dc)*

Row 4: Rep row 3 of Left Front. *(31 [33, 35, 37] dc)*

Next rows: [Rep rows 3 and 4 alternately] until 16 [18, 19, 22] rows are completed. Fasten off. *(15 [15, 16, 15] dc)*

SLEEVE
Make 2.
Row 1: With MC, work dc foundation st 29 [33, 33, 35] times, turn. *(29 [33, 33, 35] dc)*

Row 2: Rep row 2 of Back, inc 1 st at each end of 3rd row and every

RS row to 39 [43, 47, 51] sts.

Rep row 2 of Back until Sleeve measures 6 [7, 8, 8] inches from beg. Fasten off.

ASSEMBLY

Sew Fronts to Back across shoulders. For each sleeve, fold Sleeve in half lengthwise, place center of Sleeve at shoulder seam and sew Sleeve into opening. Sew Sleeve and side seams.

EDGING

Join CC with sl st in first dc of back neck after right shoulder seam, ch 1, sc in same st as beg ch-1, [ch 3, hdc in sc just made, sk next dc, sc in next dc] across back neck, working in ends of rows down Left Front, [sc in side of dc at end of next row, ch 3, hdc in sc just made] across to corner, working across foundation, sc in base of corner foundation dc, [ch 3, hdc in sc just made, sk next foundation st, sc in next foundation st] across to next corner, then working in ends of rows up Right Front, [ch 3, hdc in sc just made, sc in side of dc at end of next row] across, ch 3, hdc in last sc, join in first sc. Fasten off.

SLEEVE EDGING

Join CC in base of foundation dc after Sleeve seam, ch 1, sc in same st as joining, ch 3, hdc in top of sc just made, sk next dc, [sc in next st, ch 3, hdc in top of sc just made, sk next dc] around, join in first sc. Fasten off.

Rep Sleeve Edging on 2nd Sleeve.

FINISHING

Sew Button to inside of Right Front opposite edging at beg of neck shaping. Sew 2nd button to outside of Left Front opposite edging at beg of neck shaping. Sew 3rd button to foundation row of Left Front at bottom corner. Use ch-3 sps of Edging for natural button lps. ●

Bikini

BY **DIANE SIMPSON**

SKILL LEVEL
INTERMEDIATE

FINISHED SIZES
Instructions given fit size infant's size 9–12 months; changes for child's sizes 2 and 3 are in [ ].

MATERIALS

- Light (light worsted) weight yarn:
    - 1½ oz blue
    - ¼ oz each pink, yellow and red
    - 2 yds green
- Size E/4/3.5mm crochet hook or size needed to obtain gauge
- Tapestry needle
- Safety pin

GAUGE
5 dc = 1 inch; 5 dc rows = 2 inches; 3 dc rnds = 1½ inches

PATTERN NOTES
Weave in loose ends as work progresses.

Join rounds with slip stitch unless otherwise stated.

INSTRUCTIONS

TOP
Triangle
Make 2.
Rnd 1: Starting at center, **slip ring** *(see Foundation Stitches on page 172)*, ch 3 *(counts as first dc)*, 11 dc in slip ring, **join** *(see Pattern Notes)* in 4th ch of beg ch. *(12 dc)*

Rnd 2: Ch 3, dc in each of next 2 sts, 7 dc in next st, [dc in each of next 3 sts, 7 dc in next st] twice, join in 3rd ch of beg ch. *(30 dc)*

Rnd 3: Ch 3, dc in each of next 5 dc, 5 dc in next st, [dc in each of next 9 sts, 5 dc in next dc] twice, dc in each of next 3 dc, join in 3rd ch of beg ch. *(42 dc)*

Rnd 4: Ch 3, dc in each of next 7 dc, 5 dc in next dc, [dc in each of next 13 dc, 5 dc in next dc] twice, dc in each of next 5 dc, join in 3rd ch of beg ch. *(54 dc)*

Rnd 5: Ch 1, sc in each of next 11 sts, ch 102, sl st in 2nd ch from hook, sl st in each ch across to last sc made, sc in last sc made *(neck strap)*, sc in each of next 17 sts, (sc, hdc, 3 dc) in next st, dc in each of next 17 sts, (3 dc, hdc, sc) in next st, sc in each of next 7 sts, join in first sc, leaving a 9-inch length, fasten off.

For **casing**, fold dc of rnd 5 over and sew to bottom of sts in rnd 3.

For **tie**, with blue, ch 160 [160, 165], sc in 2nd ch from hook, sc in each rem ch across, fasten off. Attach safety pin to end of Tie, pass Tie through casing of each Triangle.

BOTTOM
Row 1: With blue, **dc foundation st** *(see Foundation Stitches on page 172)* 40 [45, 50] times, turn. *(40 [45, 50] dc)*

Row 2: Ch 3 *(counts as first dc)*, dc in each st across, turn.

Row 3: Rep row 2.

Rows 4–8: Ch 3, **dc dec** *(see Stitch Guide)* in next 2 sts, dc in each st across to last 3 sts, dc dec in next 2 sts, dc in last st, turn. *(30 [35, 40] dc at end of last row)*

Rows 9–13 [9–14, 9–15]: Ch 3, [dc dec in next 2 sts] twice, dc in each st across to last 5 sts, [dc dec in next 2 sts] twice, dc in last st, turn. *(10 [11, 12] dc at end of last row)*

Rows 14–16 [15–18, 16–20]: Rep row 2.

Rows 17–21 [19–24, 21–27]: Ch 3, 2 dc in each of next 2 sts, dc in each st across to last 3 sts, 2 dc in each of next 2 sts, dc in last st, turn. *(30 [35, 40] dc at end of last row)*

Tie
Make 2.
With blue ch 120 [120, 125], sl st in 2nd ch from hook, sl st in each rem ch across, fasten off. Attach safety pin to end of Tie, pass a Tie though each front and back casing, tie ends in a bow.

FLOWER
Make 4.
Rnd 1: With green, starting at center, **slip ring** (see Foundation Stitches on page 172), ch 1, 5 sc in slip ring, **join** (see Pattern Notes) in first sc, fasten off. (5 sc)

Rnd 2: Working in **front lps** (see Stitch Guide) of sts, join pink with sl st in any st, *(ch 3, dc, ch 3, sl st) in same st, sl st in next st, rep from * around, fasten off. (5 petals)

Rnd 3: Working in **back lps** (see Stitch Guide) of rnd 1, join yellow with sl st in any st, *(ch 4, 2 tr, ch 4, sl st) in same st, sl st in next st, rep from * around, fasten off. (5 petals)

Rnd 4: Join red with sl st in sl st between petals of rnd 3, [ch 2, sl st in sl st between next 2 petals] around. (5 ch-2 sps)

Rnd 5: *Sl st in next ch-2 sp, [(ch 4, 3 tr, ch 4, sl st) in same ch-2 sp, rep from * around, fasten off.

For Top, sew 1 Flower over rnds 2–4 above each casing of each Triangle.

For Bottom, sew 2 Flowers side by side at slight angle over rows 3–6 at top right of Bottom. ●

Rows 22–26 [25–29, 28–32]: Ch 3, 2 dc in next st, dc in each st across to last 2 sts, 2 dc in next st, dc in last st, turn. (40 [45, 50] dc at end of last row)

Rows 27–29 [30–32, 33–35]: Rep row 2. At the end of last row, fasten off.

For **casing**, fold over sts of row 29 [32, 35], sew to bottom of sts in row 27 [30, 33]. Fold over row 1 and sew to bottom of sts of row 3.

Autumn Rose Hat

BY **SANDY ABBATE**

SKILL LEVEL ■■□□ EASY

FINISHED SIZES

Instructions given fit infant's size 6 months *(small)*; changes for size 9 months *(medium)* and size 12 months *(large)* are in [ ]. When only 1 number is given, it applies to all sizes.

MATERIALS

- Red Heart Classic medium (worsted) weight yarn (3½ oz/190 yds/99g per skein):
  - 1 skein #336 warm brown
  - 1 oz #902 jockey red
  - 1/4 oz #686 paddy green
- Sizes F/5/3.75mm, G/6/4mm and H/8/5mm crochet hooks or sizes needed to obtain gauge
- Tapestry needle

GAUGES

Size F hook for size small: 4 dc = 1 inch; 2 dc rnds = 1 inch

Size G hook for size medium: 7 dc = 2 inches; 6 dc rnds = 3½ inches

Size H hook for size large: 3 dc = 1 inch; 5 dc rnds = 3 inches

PATTERN NOTES

Weave in loose ends as work progresses.

Join rounds with slip stitch unless otherwise stated.

SPECIAL STITCH

3-double crochet cluster (3-dc cl): [Yo, draw up a lp in next st, yo, draw through 2 lps on hook] 3 times, yo, draw through rem 4 lps on hook.

INSTRUCTIONS

HAT

Rnd 1: Starting at top of Hat with warm brown, work **slip ring** *(see Foundation Stitches on page 172)*, ch 3 *(counts as first dc)*, 11 dc in slip ring, **join** *(see Pattern Notes)* in 3rd ch of beg ch. *(12 dc)*

Rnd 2: Ch 3, dc in same st as beg ch, 2 dc in each dc around, join in 3rd ch of beg ch. *(24 dc)*

Rnd 3: Ch 3, dc in same st as beg ch, dc in next st, [2 dc in next st, dc in next st] around, join in 3rd ch of beg ch. *(36 dc)*

Rnd 4: Ch 3, dc in same st as beg ch, dc in each of next 2 sts, [2 dc in next st, dc in each of next 2 sts] around, join in 3rd ch of beg ch. *(48 dc)*

Rnd 5: Ch 3, dc in same st as beg ch, dc in each of next 3 sts, [2 dc in next st, dc in each of next 3 sts] around, join in 3rd ch of beg ch. *(60 dc)*

Rnds 6–10: Ch 3, dc in each st around, join in 3rd ch of beg ch.

Rnd 11: Ch 3, dc in same st as beg ch, dc in each of next 4 sts, [2 dc in next st, dc in each of next 4 sts] around, join in 3rd ch of beg ch. *(72 dc)*

Rnd 12: Ch 3, dc in same st as beg ch, dc in each of next 5 sts, [2 dc in next st, dc in each of next 5 sts] around, join in 3rd ch of beg ch. *(84 dc)*

Rnd 13: Ch 3, dc in same st as beg ch, dc in each of next 6 sts, [2 dc in next st, dc in each of next 6 sts] around, join in 3rd ch of beg ch. *(96 dc)*

Rnd 14: Ch 1, **reverse sc** *(see Fig. 1)* in each st around, join in beg reverse sc, fasten off.

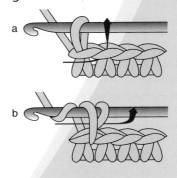

Fig. 1
Reverse Single Crochet

CONTINUED ON PAGE 142

T-Strap Booties

BY **YVONNE HEALY**

SKILL LEVEL
EASY

FINISHED SIZE
Newborn to 6 months

MATERIALS
- Red Heart LusterSheen fine (sport) weight yarn (4 oz/335 yds/113g per skein): 1 skein #0235 think pink
- Size D/3/3.25mm crochet hook or size needed to obtain gauge
- Tapestry needle
- Sewing needle and thread
- 2 white 8mm buttons

GAUGE
5 dc = 1 inch

PATTERN NOTES
Weave in loose ends as work progresses.

Join rounds with slip stitch unless otherwise stated.

INSTRUCTIONS

SOLE
Make 2.
Rnd 1: Work **dc foundation st** *(see Foundation Stitches on page 172)* 11 times, dc foundation st 4 times in same st, working on opposite side of foundation ch, dc in each of next 10 chs, **join** *(see Pattern Notes)* in first dc foundation st. *(26 dc)*

Rnd 2: Ch 3 *(counts as first dc throughout)*, dc in each of next 11 dc, 2 dc in each of next 5 dc, dc in each of next 8 dc, 2 dc in next dc, join in 3rd ch of beg ch. *(32 dc)*

Rnd 3: Ch 3, dc in same st as beg ch-3, dc in each of next 13 dc, [2 dc in next dc, dc in next dc] 3 times, dc in each of next 11 dc, 2 dc in next dc, join in 3rd ch of beg ch-3. *(37 dc)*

Rnd 4: Ch 2 *(counts as first hdc)*, working in **back lps** *(see Stitch Guide)* for this rnd only, hdc in each st around, join in 2nd ch of beg ch-2.

Rnd 5: Ch 2, hdc in each hdc around, join in 2nd of beg ch, fasten off.

UPPER TOE
Row 1: Ch 1, counting sts toward Toe section of Bootie,

CONTINUED ON PAGE 143

Cupcake Hat & Purse

BY **DARLA SIMS**

SKILL LEVEL ■■■□ INTERMEDIATE

FINISHED SIZES

Hat: Instructions given fit children ages 4–10 years, measuring 18–20 inches in diameter

Purse: Base measures 4½ inches in diameter, bottom to top 7½ inches, excluding Ties

MATERIALS

- Red Heart Soft Yarn medium (worsted) weight yarn (5 oz/256 yds/140g per skein):
     1 skein each #4600 white *(MC)*, #6768 pink *(A)*, #9344 chocolate *(B)* and #4420 guacamole *(C)*
- Sizes G/6/4mm and H/8/5mm crochet hook or sizes needed to obtain gauge
- Tapestry needle
- Stitch marker

GAUGES

Size H hook: 7 sc = 2 inches; 5 sc rnds = 1½ inches

Size G hook: 4 sc = 1 inch; 6 sc rows = 1½ inches

PATTERN NOTES

Weave in loose ends as work progresses.

Join rounds with slip stitch unless otherwise stated.

SPECIAL STITCH

Popcorn (pc): Work 5 dc in indicated st, draw up lp, remove hook, insert hook in first dc of 5-dc group, pick up dropped lp and draw through st on hook.

INSTRUCTIONS

PURSE
Bottom
Rnd 1: Starting at center

Bottom, with size H hook and MC, work **slip ring** *(see Foundation Stitches on page 172)*, 8 sc in slip ring, do not join rnds, use st marker to mark rnds. *(8 sc)*

Rnd 2: Work 2 sc in each sc around. *(16 sc)*

Rnd 3: [Sc in next sc, 2 sc in next sc] around. *(24 sc)*

Rnd 4: [Sc in each of next 2 sc, 2 sc in next sc] around. *(32 sc)*

Rnd 5: [Sc in each of next 3 sc, 2 sc in next sc] around. *(40 sc)*

Rnd 6: [Sc in each of next 4 sc, 2 sc in next sc] around. *(48 sc)*

Rnd 7: [Sc in each of next 5 sc, 2 sc in next sc] around. *(56 sc)*

Sides
Row 1: Now working in rows around Bottom, ch 8, sc in 2nd ch from hook, sc in each of next 6 chs, sl st in end st of next sc of Bottom, sl st in next sc, turn.

Row 2: Working in **back lps** *(see Stitch Guide)*, sk next 2 sl sts of rnd 7 of Bottom, sc in each of next 7 sts of Sides, turn.

Row 3: Ch 1, working in back lps only, sc in each of next 7 sts, sl st in each of next 2 sc of Rnd 7 of Bottom, turn.

Rows 4–56: Rep rows 2 and 3. At the end of last rep, with RS facing, working through both lps, holding last row to opposite side of row 1, sl st across sts, fasten off.

Icing Ruffle
Rnd 1: Working in side edge of sc sts of Sides, with size H hook, join A with sl st in end of row, ch 1, work 56 sc around, join in beg sc, **do not turn**. *(56 sc)*

Rnd 2: Ch 1, working in back lps only, sc in each st around, join in beg sc, turn.

Rnd 3: Working in rem lps of rnd 1, sl st into rem lp, ch 3 *(counts as first dc)*, 2 dc in same st as beg ch, 3 dc in each rem st around, join in 3rd ch of beg ch, fasten off.

Rnd 4: Join B with sl st in any sc of rnd 2, ch 2 *(counts as first hdc)*, hdc in each sc around, join in 2nd ch of beg ch.

Rnd 5: Ch 2, hdc in each st around, join in 2nd ch of beg ch.

Rnd 6: Rep rnd 5, fasten off.

Rnd 7: Join C with sc in any st of rnd 6, sc in each of next 2 sc, (sc, ch 5, sc) in next sc, [sc in each of next 3 sc, (sc, ch 5, sc) in next sc] around, join in beg sc, fasten off. *(14 ch-5 lps)*

Rnd 8: Join A with sc in first sc of previous rnd, **pc** *(see Special Stitch)* in next sc, sc in next sc, sk each of next sc, ch-5 and next sc, sc in next sc, [pc in next sc, sc in next sc, sk each of next sc, ch-5 and next sc] around, join in beg sc, fasten off. *(14 pc)*

Rnd 9: Join B with sl st in first sc of previous rnd, ch 2, hdc in pc, hdc in next sc, hdc in sp after last sc directly above ch-5 sp 2 rnds below, [hdc in next sc, hdc in pc, hdc in next sc, hdc in sp after last sc directly above ch-5 sp 2 rnds below] around, join in 2nd ch of beg ch. *(56 hdc)*

Rnds 10–13: Ch 2, hdc in each st around, join in 2nd ch of beg ch. *(56 hdc)*

Rnd 14: Ch 4 *(counts as first dc, ch 1)*, sk next hdc, [dc in next hdc, ch 1, sk next hdc] around, join in 3rd ch of beg ch-4. *(28 ch-1 sps)*

Rnd 15: Ch 2, [dc in next ch-1 sp, dc in next dc] around, join in 2nd ch of beg ch, fasten off. *(56 dc)*

Rnd 16: Join A with sc in any st, tr in next st, [sc in next st, tr in next st] around, join in beg sc, fasten off.

Tie
Make 2.
With size H hook and C, make a ch 19 inches long, sl st in 2nd ch from hook, sl st in each rem ch across, fasten off.

Weave first Tie through ch-1 sps of rnd 14, sew ends tog; starting at opposite edge, weave 2nd Tie through ch-1 sps opposite of previous weave, sew ends tog. Holding a tie in each hand pull gently to close Purse.

HAT
Ribbing
Row 1: With size G hook and MC, **sc foundation st** *(see Foundation Stitches on page 172)* 10 times, turn. *(10 sc)*

Row 2: Ch 1, working in **back**

lps *(see Stitch Guide)*, sc in each st across, turn.

Rows 3–60: Rep row 2. At the end of last rep, holding last row to opposite side of row 1 and working through both thicknesses, sl st across, fasten off.

Icing Ruffle
Rnd 1: Working in ends of rows of Ribbing, attach A with sc, sc in each row around, **join** *(see Pattern Notes)* in beg sc. *(60 sc)*

Rnd 2: Ch 1, working in **back lps** *(see Stitch Guide)*, sc in each st around, join in beg sc, turn.

Rnd 3: Working in rem lps of rnd 1, ch 3, 2 dc in same st as beg ch, 3 dc in each st around, join in 3rd ch of beg ch, fasten off.

Body of Hat
Rnd 4: With size H hook, attach B with sl st in any st of rnd 2, ch 2, hdc in each st around, join in 2nd ch of beg ch. *(60 hdc)*

Rnds 5 & 6: Ch 2, hdc in each st around, join in 2nd ch of beg ch.

Rnd 7: Rep rnd 7 of Icing Ruffle of Purse. *(15 ch-5 lps)*

Rnd 8: Rep rnd 8 of Icing Ruffle of Purse. *(15 pc)*

Rnd 9: Rep rnd 9 of Icing Ruffle of Purse. *(60 hdc)*

Rnds 10–12: Ch 2, hdc in next st, [hdc dec in next 2 sts, hdc in next st] around, join in 2nd ch of beg ch.

Rnd 13: Ch 4, sk next st, [dc in

next st, ch 1, sk next st] around, join in 3rd ch of beg ch-4.

Rnd 14: Ch 1, sc in each dc and in each ch-1 sp around, join in beg sc, fasten off.

Rnd 15: Join A with sc in any sc, tr in next st, [sc in next st, tr in next st] around, join in beg sc, fasten off.

Tie
With size H hook and C, make a ch 15 inches in length, sl st in 2nd ch from hook, sl st in each rem ch across, fasten off.

Weave through ch-1 sps of rnd 13, pull to close opening, tie ends in a bow. ●

Spiral Popcorn Baby Blanket

BY **DIANE SIMPSON**

SKILL LEVEL ■■■□
INTERMEDIATE

FINISHED SIZE
36½ inches in diameter, excluding 2½-inch Ruffle

MATERIALS
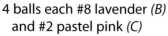

- Plymouth Heaven bulky (chunky) weight yarn (1¾ oz/55 yds/50g per ball):
  - 9 balls #9 white *(A)*
  - 4 balls each #8 lavender *(B)* and #2 pastel pink *(C)*
- Size K/10½/6.5mm crochet hook or size needed to obtain gauge
- Yarn needle
- Stitch marker

GAUGE
8 dc = 4 inches; 4 dc rnds = 4 inches

PATTERN NOTES
Weave in loose ends as work progresses.

Spiral created by working from 4 separate balls of yarn.

Stitch marker is used in first stitch of each round to make sure the same round ends in stitch before first stitch. Move marker as work progresses.

SPECIAL STITCH
Popcorn (pc): 5 dc in indicated st, draw up a lp, remove hook, insert hook in first dc of 5-dc group, pick up dropped lp and draw through lp on hook, ch 1 to lock.

INSTRUCTIONS

BLANKET
Rnd 1: Starting at center with C, work **slip ring** *(see Foundation Stitches on page 172)* *ch 1, (sc, hdc, dc) in slip ring, draw up a lp on hook to about 4 inches, drop lp from hook*, join A with sl st in same sl ring, rep from * to *, join B with sl st in same slip ring, rep from * to *, join 2nd ball of A with sl st in same slip ring, rep from * to *, tighten slip ring and secure. *(12 sts)*

Rnd 2: Pick up next dropped C lp, tighten lp around hook, dc in first st of next color, mark st just completed with st marker, dc in same st, 2 dc in each of next 2 sts, draw up 4-inch lp, remove lp from hook, *pick up dropped lp of next color, tighten yarn to hook, 2 dc in each of next 3 sts, draw up 4-inch lp, remove lp from hook, rep from * twice. *(24 dc)*

Rnd 3: Pick up next dropped C lp, tighten lp around hook, dc in first st of next color, mark st just made, 2 dc in next st, [dc in next st, 2 dc in next st] twice, draw up 4-inch lp, remove lp from hook, *pick up dropped lp of next color, tighten yarn to hook, [dc in next st, 2 dc in next st] 3 times, draw up 4-inch lp, drop lp from hook, rep from * twice. *(36 dc)*

Rnd 4: Pick up next dropped C lp, tighten lp around hook, dc in first st of next color, mark st just completed, dc in next st, 2 dc in next st, [dc in each of next 2 sts, 2 dc in next st] twice, draw up 4-inch lp, drop lp from hook, *pick up dropped lp of next color, tighten lp around hook, [dc in each of next 2 sts, 2 dc in next st] 3 times, draw up 4-inch lp, drop lp from hook, rep from * twice. *(48 dc)*

Rnd 5: Pick up next dropped C lp, tighten lp around hook, dc in first st of next color, mark st

CONTINUED ON PAGE 143

Baby Blue Blanket

BY **LUCILLE LAFLAMME**

SKILL LEVEL

■■■□ INTERMEDIATE

FINISHED SIZE
34 x 40 inches

MATERIALS

- Red Heart Soft Baby light (light worsted) weight yarn (7 oz/575 yds/198g per skein):
    2 skeins #7881 powder blue
- Size G/6/4mm crochet hook or size needed to obtain gauge
- Yarn needle

GAUGE
4 dc = 1 inch; 2 dc rows = 1 inch

PATTERN NOTES
Weave in loose ends as work progresses.

Join rounds with slip stitch unless otherwise stated.

SPECIAL STITCHES
Picot: Ch 3, sl st in top of cl or indicated st.

Cluster (cl): [Yo, insert hook in next dc, yo, draw up lp, yo, draw through 2 lps on hook] 3 times, yo, draw through all 4 lps on hook.

INSTRUCTIONS

BLANKET
Row 1: Starting at bottom edge of Blanket, work **dc foundation st** *(see Foundation Stitches on page 172)* 130 times, turn. *(130 dc)*

Row 2: Ch 3 *(counts as first dc)*, dc in each dc across, turn.

Row 3: Rep row 2.

Row 4: Ch 3, dc in each of next 6 dc, ch 5, [sk next 5 dc, dc in each of next 2 dc, ch 4, sk next 5 dc, (dc, ch 1, 2 dc, ch 1, dc) in next dc, ch 4] 8 times, sk next 5 dc, dc in each of next 2 dc, ch 5, sk next 5 dc, dc in each of next 7 dc, turn.

Row 5: Ch 3, dc in each of next 6 dc, ch 3, sc in next ch-5 sp, ch 3, dc in each of next 2 dc, [ch 3, 3 dc in next dc, ch 2, dc in each of next 2 dc, ch 2, 3 dc in next dc, ch 3, dc in each of next 2 dc] 8 times, ch 3, sc in next ch-5 sp, ch 3, dc in each of next 7 dc, turn.

Row 6: Ch 3, dc in each of next 6 dc, ch 5, dc in each of next 2 dc, [ch 2, **cl** *(see Special Stitches)* in next 3 dc, **picot** *(see Special Stitches)* in top of last cl, ch 3,

(dc, ch 1, dc) in each of next 2 dc, ch 3, cl in next 3 dc, picot in top of last ch, ch 2, dc in each of next 2 dc] 8 times, ch 5, dc in each of next 7 dc, turn.

Rows 7–78: [Rep rows 5 and 6 alternately] 36 times.

Row 79: Ch 3, dc in each of next 6 dc, [ch 5, sk next ch-5 sp, dc in each of next 2 dc, ch 5, sk next cl and picot, sk next (dc, ch 1, dc), dc in sp between next 2 dc, sk next (dc, ch 1, dc), ch 5, sk next cl and picot, dc in each of next 2 dc] 8 times, ch 5, dc in each of next 7 dc, turn.

Row 80: Ch 3, dc in each dc and each ch across, turn.

Rows 81 & 82: Rep row 2. At the end of row 82, **do not turn**.

BORDER
Rnd 83: *[Ch 6, sl st in 4th ch from hook, ch 3, sl st in end st of every other row down] to next corner, picot in corner st, [ch 6, sl st in 4th ch from hook, ch 3, sk next 4 sts, sl st in next st] to next corner, picot in corner st, rep from * around, sl st in first st. Fasten off. ●

Little Garden Coat

BY **LISA PFLUG**

SKILL LEVEL
INTERMEDIATE

FINISHED SIZES
Instructions given fit infant's size 6–12 months; changes for size 12–18 months and size 18–24 months are in [ ]. When only 1 number is given, it applies to all sizes.

FINISHED GARMENT MEASUREMENTS
Chest: 20½ inches *(6–12 months)* [22 inches *(12–18 months)*, 23½ inches *(18–24 months)*]

MATERIALS

MEDIUM
- Caron Simply Soft Heather medium (worsted) weight yarn (5 oz/250 yds/142g per skein):
    2 skeins #9503 woodland heather *(A)*
    10 yards #9505 plum heather *(C)*
- Caron Simply Soft medium (worsted) weight yarn (3 oz/157 yds/85g per skein):
    1 skein #2614 soft pink *(B)*
- Size I/9/5.5mm crochet hook or size needed to obtain gauge
- Yarn needle
- Stitch markers
- 3 pearl 18mm heart-shaped buttons

GAUGE
[Sc in next st, dc in next st] 6 times = 4 inches; 6 rows = 2 inches

PATTERN NOTES
Weave in loose ends as work progresses.

Join rounds with slip stitch unless otherwise stated.

INSTRUCTIONS

BODY
Row 1: Starting at bottom edge with A, work **dc foundation st** *(see Foundation Stitches on page 172)*, [**sc foundation st** *(see Foundation Stitches on page 172)*, dc foundation st] 29 [31, 33] times, turn. *(59 [63, 67] sts)*

Row 2: Ch 1, sc in first dc, [dc in next sc, sc in next dc] across, turn. *(59 [63, 67] sts)*

Row 3: Ch 2 *(counts as first dc)*, [sc in next dc, dc in next sc] across, turn.

Rows 4–19 [4–21, 4–25]: [Rep rows 2 and 3 alternately] 8 [9, 11] times.

Row 20 [22, 26]: Rep row 2. At the end of row, place st marker on 15th [16th, 17th] st of row and mark as RS.

LEFT FRONT
For Size 6–12 Months Only
Row 1: Ch 2, [sc in next dc, dc in next sc] 6 times, sc in next dc, turn. *(14 sts)*

Row 2: Ch 1, sk first sc, [sc in next dc, dc in next sc] 6 times, sc in next dc, turn. *(13 sts)*

Row 3: Ch 2 [sc in next dc, dc in next sc] 6 times, turn.

Row 4: Ch 1, sc in first dc, [dc in next sc, sc in next dc] 6 times, turn.

Rows 5 & 6: Rep rows 3 and 4.

Row 7: Sk first st, sl st in each of next 3 sts, ch 1, sc in same st as last sl st, [dc in next sc, sc in next dc] 4 times, dc in last st, turn. *(10 sts)*

Row 8: Ch 1, sc in first dc, [dc in next sc, sc in next dc] 4 times, leaving rem st unworked, turn. *(9 sts)*

Row 9: Ch 2, [sc in next dc, dc in next sc] 4 times, turn.

Row 10: Ch 1, sc in first dc, [dc in next sc, sc in next dc] 4 times, turn.

Row 11: Rep row 9. Fasten off.

For Size 12–18 Months Only

Row [1]: Ch 2, [sc in next dc, dc in next sc] [7] times, turn. ([15] sts)

Row [2]: Ch 1, sk first st, [dc in next sc, sc in next dc] [7] times, turn. ([14] sts)

Row [3]: Ch 2, [sc in next dc, dc in next sc] [6] times, sc in next dc, turn.

Rows [4–8]: Rep row [3].

Row [9]: Sk first st, sl st in each of next 3 sts, ch 1, sc in same st as last sl st, [dc in next sc, sc in next dc] [5] times, turn. ([11] sts)

Row [10]: Ch 2, [sc in next dc, dc in next sc] [4] times, sc in next dc, leaving rem st unworked, turn. ([10] sts)

Row [11]: Ch 2, [sc in next dc, dc in next sc] [4] times, sc in next dc, turn. ([10] sts)

Rows [12 & 13]: Rep row [10]. Fasten off.

For Size 18–24 Months Only

Row [1]: Ch 2, [sc in next dc, dc in next sc] [7] times, sc in next dc, turn. ([16] sts)

Row [2]: Ch 1, sk first sc, [sc in next dc, dc in next sc] [7] times, sc in next dc, turn. ([15] sts)

Row [3]: Ch 2, [sc in next dc, dc in next sc] [6] times, sc in next dc, leaving rem st unworked, turn. ([14] sts)

Row [4]: Ch 2, [sc in next dc, dc in next sc] [6] times, sc in next dc, turn.

Rows [5–10]: Rep row [4].

Row [11]: Sk first st, sl st in each of next 3 sts, ch 1, sc in same st as last sl st, [dc in next sc, sc in next dc] [5] times, turn. ([11] sts)

Row [12]: Ch 2, [sc in next dc, dc in next sc] [4] times, sc in next dc, leaving rem st unworked, turn. ([10] sts)

Row [13]: Ch 2, [sc in next dc, dc in next sc] [4] times, sc in next dc, turn.

Rows [14 & 15]: Rep row [13]. Fasten off.

RIGHT FRONT
For All Sizes

With WS of row 20 [22, 26] facing, attach A with sl st to st left of marked st.

For Size 6–12 Months Only

Row 1: Ch 1, sc in same st, [dc in next sc, sc in next dc] 6 times, dc in next sc, turn. (14 sts)

Row 2: Ch 1, sc in same st, [dc in next sc, sc in next dc] 6 times, leaving rem st unworked, turn. (13 sts)

Row 3: Ch 2, [sc in next dc, dc in next sc] 6 times, turn.

Row 4: Ch 1, sc in same st, [dc in next sc, sc in next dc] 6 times, turn.

Rows 5 & 6: Rep rows 3 and 4.

Row 7: Ch 2, [sc in next dc, dc in next sc] 4 times, sc in next dc, leaving rem 3 sts unworked, turn. (10 sts)

Row 8: Ch 1, sk first st, [sc in next st, dc in next st] 4 times, sc in next dc, turn. (9 sts)

Row 9: Ch 2, [sc in next dc, dc in next sc] 4 times, turn.

Row 10: Ch 1, sc in same st, [dc in next sc, sc in next dc] 4 times, turn.

Row 11: Rep row 9. Fasten off.

For Size 12–18 Months Only

Row [1]: Ch 2, [sc in next dc, dc in next sc] [7] times, turn. ([15] sts)

Row [2]: Ch 1, sc in same st, [dc in next sc, sc in next dc] [6] times, dc in next sc, leaving rem st unworked, turn. ([14] sts)

Row [3]: Ch 1, sc in same st, [dc in next sc, sc in next dc] [6] times, dc in next sc, turn.

Rows [4–8]: Rep row [3].

Row [9]: Ch 1, sc in same st, [dc in next sc, sc in next dc] [5] times, leaving rem 3 sts unworked, turn. ([11] sts)

Row [10]: Ch 1, sk first st, [sc in next dc, dc in next sc] [5] times, turn. ([10] dc)

Row [11]: Ch 1, sc in same st, [dc in next sc, sc in next dc] [4] times, dc in next sc, turn.

Rows [12 & 13]: Rep row [11].

Fasten off.

For Size 18–24 Months Only

Row [1]: Ch 1, sc in same st, [dc in next sc, sc in next dc] [7] times, dc in next sc, turn. *([16] sts)*

Row [2]: Ch 1, sc in same st, [dc in next sc, sc in next dc] [7] times, leaving rem st unworked, turn. *([15] sts)*

Row [3]: Ch 1, sk first st, [sc in next dc, dc in next sc] [7] times, turn. *([14] sts)*

Row [4]: Ch 1, sc in same st, [dc in next sc, sc in next dc] [6] times, dc in next sc, turn.

Rows [5–10]: Rep row [4].

Row [11]: Ch 1, sc in same st, [dc in next sc, sc in next dc] [5] times, leaving rem 3 sts unworked, turn. *([11] sts)*

Row [12]: Ch 1, sk first st, [sc in next dc, dc in next sc] [5] times, turn. *([10] sts)*

Row [13]: Ch 1, sc in same st, [dc in next sc, sc in next dc] [4] times, dc in next sc, turn.

Rows [14 & 15]: Rep row [9]. Fasten off.

BACK
For All Sizes
With WS of row 20 [22, 26] facing, attach A at first unworked st.

For Size 6–12 Months Only
Row 1: Ch 2, [sc in next dc, dc in next sc] 15 times, turn. *(31 sts)*

Row 2: Ch 1, sk first st, [dc in next sc, sc in next dc] 14 times, dc in next sc, leaving rem st unworked, turn. *(29 sts)*

Row 3: Ch 1, sc in same st, [dc in next sc, sc in next dc] 14 times, turn.

Row 4: Ch 2, [sc in first dc, dc in next sc] 14 times, turn.

Rows 5–10: [Rep rows 3 and 4 alternately] 3 times.

Row 11: Rep row 3. Fasten off.

For Size 12–18 Months Only
Row [1]: Ch 1, sc in same st, [dc in next sc, sc in next dc] [16] times, turn. *([33] sts)*

Row [2]: Ch 1, sk first st, [sc in next dc, dc in next sc] [15] times, sc in next dc, leaving rem st unworked, turn. *([31] sts)*

Row [3]: Ch 2, [sc in next dc, dc in next sc] [15] times, turn.

Row [4]: Ch 1, sc in same st, [dc in next sc, sc in next dc] [15] times, turn.

Rows [5, 7, 9, 11]: Rep row [3].

Rows [6, 8, 10, 12]: Rep row [4]. Fasten off.

For Size 18–24 Months Only
Row [1]: Ch 2, [sc in next dc, dc in next sc] [17] times, turn. *([35] sts)*

Row [2]: Ch 1, sk first st, [dc in next sc, sc in next dc] [16] times, dc in next sc, leaving rem st unworked, turn. *([33] sts)*

Row [3]: Ch 1, sk first st, [dc in next sc, sc in next dc] [15] times, dc in next sc, leaving rem st unworked, turn. *([31] sts)*

Row [4]: Ch 2, [sc in next dc, dc in next sc] [15] times, turn.

Row [5]: Ch 1, sc in same st, [dc in next sc, sc in next dc] [15] times, turn.

Rows [6, 8, 10, 12]: Rep rows [4] and 5 alternately] [5] times.

Rows [7, 9, 11, 13]: Rep row [5]. Fasten off.

SLEEVE
For All Sizes
Make 2.
Row 1: Starting at bottom edge with A, work dc foundation st, [sc foundation st, c foundation st] 9 [10, 11] times, turn. *(19 [21, 23] sts)*

Row 2: Ch 1, sc in same st, [dc in next sc, sc in next dc] 9 [10, 11] times, turn.

Row 3: Ch 2, [sc in next dc, dc in next sc] 9 [10, 11] times, turn.

Row 4: Ch 2, sc in same st as beg ch-2, [dc in next sc, sc in next dc] 9 [10, 11] times, dc in same st as last sc, turn. *(21 [23, 25] sts)*

Row 5: Ch 1, sc in same st, [dc in next sc, sc in next dc] 10 [11, 12] times, turn.

CONTINUED ON PAGE 144

Peekins Summer Dress

BY **JOYCE NORDSTROM**

SKILL LEVEL ◼◼◼◻
INTERMEDIATE

FINISHED SIZES
Instructions given fit infant's size 6–9 months; changes size 9–12 months are in [ ]. When only 1 number is given, it applies to both sizes.

FINISHED GARMENT MEASUREMENTS
Chest: 18 inches (*size 6–9 months*) [19 inches (*size 9–12 months*)]

MATERIALS
- Aunt Lydia's Fashion Crochet size 3 crochet cotton (150 yds per ball): 11 [12, 13] balls #226 natural
- Size D/3/3.25mm crochet hook or size needed to obtain gauge
- Yarn needle
- 4 natural ½-inch shank buttons
- Stitch marker

GAUGE
[Ch 1, sk next st, dc] 3 times = 1 inch; 3 dc rows = 1½ inches

PATTERN NOTES
Weave in loose ends as work progresses.

Join rounds with slip stitch unless otherwise stated.

Dress yoke is worked from waist to shoulders and skirt is worked from waist down.

SPECIAL STITCHES
Beginning open block (beg open block): Ch 4 (*counts as first dc, ch 1*).

Open block: Ch 1, sk 1 st, dc in next st.

Cluster (cl): Worked only in a ch-1 sp; [yo, draw up lp in ch-1 sp, yo, draw through 2 lps on hook] 3 times, yo, draw through all 4 lps on hook, ch 1 to secure.

Beginning shell (beg shell): Ch 3, (dc, ch 1, 2 dc) in indicated st.

Shell: (2 dc, ch 1, 2 dc) in indicated st.

Beginning double shell (beg double shell): Ch 3, (dc, ch 1, 2 dc, ch 1, 2 dc) in indicated st.

Double shell: (2 dc, ch 1) twice and 2 dc in indicated st.

V-stitch (V-st): (Dc, ch 1, dc) in indicated st.

Picot: Ch 3, sl st in first ch of ch-3.

Picot shell: (2 dc, picot, 2 dc) in indicated st.

INSTRUCTIONS

BODICE
Foundation row: Starting at waistline and working upward, work **dc, ch-1 foundation** (*see Foundation Stitches on page 172*) 55 [57] times, turn.

Row 1 (RS): Beg open block (*see Special Stitches*), work **open block** (*see Foundation Stitches on page 172*) 26 [27] times, **cl** (*see Special Stitches*) in next ch-1 sp, dc in next dc, work open block 27 [28] times, turn.

Row 2: Beg open block, open block 25 [26] times, cl in next ch-1 sp, dc in next dc, ch 8, dc in next dc, cl in next ch-1 sp, dc in next dc, work open block 26 [27] times, turn.

Row 3: Beg open block, work open block 24 [25] times, cl in

next ch-1 sp, dc in next dc, ch 4, sc in center of ch-8 sp, ch 4, dc in next dc, cl in next ch-1 sp, dc in next dc, work open block 25 [26] times, turn.

Left Back
Row 4 (RS): Beg open block, work open block 11 times, leaving rem sts unworked, turn. *(12 open blocks)*

Row 5: Beg open block, work open blocks across, turn. *(12 open blocks)*

Row 6: Beg open block, work open blocks across row, ch 1, dc in same st as last dc *(open block inc at armhole edge)*, turn. *(13 open blocks)*

Row 7: Beg open block, work open block across, turn. *(13 open blocks)*

Rep row 7 until 3 inches from beg of Left Back, ending with a WS row, turn. Fasten off.

Shoulder Shaping
Row 8: Sk first 5 open blocks, join natural with sl st in next dc, beg open block, work 7 open blocks across, turn. *(8 open blocks)*

Row 9: Beg open block, work 7 open blocks across, turn.

Rep row 9 until 4 [4½] inches from beg of Left Back. Fasten off.

Front
Row 4 (RS): Sk next 3 [4] open blocks from Left Back, join natural in next dc, beg open

block, work 8 open blocks, cl in next ch-1 sp, dc in next dc, ch 5, 3 sc in next sc, ch 5, sk next ch-4 sp, sk next cl, dc in next dc, cl in next ch-1 sp, dc in next dc, work 8 open blocks, leaving rem sts unworked, turn.

Row 5: Ch 4 *(counts as first dc, ch-1)*, dc in same dc as beg ch-4 *(open block inc)*, work 8 open blocks, cl in next ch-1 sp, dc in next dc, ch 8, sk next cl, sk next ch-5 sp, 2 sc in next sc, sc in next sc, 2 sc in next sc, ch 6, sk next ch-5 sp, sk next cl, dc in next dc, cl in next ch-1 sp, dc in next dc, work 8 open blocks, ch 1, dc in same dc as last dc *(open block inc)*, turn.

Row 6: Beg open block, work 9 open blocks, cl in first ch of ch-8, dc in 6th ch of same ch-8, ch 6, sk next sc, sc in each of next 3 sc, ch 6, sk next 5 chs of ch-8, dc in next ch, cl in last ch of same ch-8, dc in next dc, work 10 open blocks, turn.

Row 7: Beg open block, work 10 open blocks, cl in next ch-6, dc in 5th ch of same ch-6, ch 6, sk next sc, sc in next sc, ch 6, sk next 4 chs of ch-6, dc in next ch of same ch-6, cl in same ch-6, dc in next dc, work 11 open blocks, turn.

Row 8: Beg open block, work 11 open blocks, cl in next ch-6, dc in 5th ch of same ch-6, ch 1, sk next sc, sk next 4 chs of next ch-6 sp, dc in next ch, cl in same ch-6, dc in next dc, work 12 open blocks, turn.

Row 9: Beg open block, work

12 open blocks, cl in next ch-1 sp, dc in next dc, work 13 open blocks, turn.

Left Shoulder Shaping
Row 10: Beg open block, work 6 open blocks across, leaving rem sts unworked, turn. *(7 open blocks)*

Row 11: Beg open block, work 6 open blocks across, turn.

Rep row 11 until same measurement as Left Back. Fasten off.

Right Shoulder Shaping
Row 10 (RS): Sk next 6 open blocks, sk next cl and next 6 open blocks *(front neck opening)*, join natural with sl st in next dc, beg open block, work 6 open blocks, turn.

Row 11: Beg open block, work across 6 open blocks, turn.

Rep row 11 until Front reaches same measurement as Left Back.

Right Back
Row 4 (RS): Sk next 3 [4] open blocks from Front, join natural with sl st in next dc, beg open block, work 11 open blocks across, turn. *(12 open blocks)*

Row 5: Beg open block, work 11 open blocks across, turn.

Row 6: Ch 4, dc in same st as beg ch-4 *(open block inc)*, work 12 open blocks across, turn. *(13 open blocks)*

Row 7: Beg open block, work

12 open blocks across, turn. *(13 open blocks)*

Rep row 7 until 3 inches from beg of Right Back ending with a WS row, turn.

Shoulder Shaping
Row 8: Beg open block, work 7 open blocks across, turn. *(8 open blocks)*

Row 9: Beg open block, work 7 open blocks across, turn.

Rep row 9 until 4 [4½] inches from beg of Right Back. Fasten off.

Sew shoulder seams; tack lower edges of center back tog.

SKIRT
Rnd 1: Holding Bodice upside down, join natural with sl st in first open block to the left of joining on Right Back, work **beg shell** *(see Special Stitches)* in same ch-1 sp, *ch 3, sk next [dc, ch-1] twice, **V-st** *(see Special Stitches)* in next dc, ch 3, sk next [ch-1, dc] twice**, shell in next ch-1 sp of open block, rep from * 10 times, ending last rep at **; *(for size 9–12 months, sk extra open block at end)*, **join** *(see Pattern Notes)* in 3rd ch of beg ch-3, **do not turn rnds.** *(11 shells, 11 V-sts)*

Rnd 2: Sl st in ch-1 sp of beg shell, beg shell in same ch-1 sp, *ch 3, 6 dc in ch-1 sp of next V-st, ch 3**, shell in ch-1 sp of next shell, rep from * around, ending last rep at **, join in 3rd ch of beg ch-3.

Rnd 3: Sl st in ch-1 sp of beg shell, beg shell in same ch-1 sp, *ch 3, dc in first dc of 6-dc group, [ch 3, dc in next dc] 5 times, ch 3**, shell in ch-1 sp of next shell, rep from * around, ending last rep at **, join in 3rd ch of beg ch-3.

Rnd 4: Sl st in ch-1 sp of beg shell, beg shell in same ch-1 sp, *ch 3, sk next ch-3 sp, sc in next ch-3 sp, [ch 3, sc in next ch-3 sp] 4 times, ch 3, sk next ch-3 sp**, shell in next ch-1 sp of shell, rep from * around, ending last rep at **, join in 3rd ch of beg ch-3.

Rnd 5: Sl st in ch-1 sp of beg shell, **beg double shell** *(see Special Stitches)* in same ch-1 sp, *ch 3, sk next ch-3 sp, sc in next ch-3 sp, [ch 3, sc in next ch-3 sp] 3 times, ch 3, sk next ch-3 sp**, **double shell** *(see Special Stitches)* in ch-1 sp of next shell, rep from * around, ending last rep at **, join in 3rd ch of beg ch-3.

Rnd 6: Sl st in ch-1 sp of beg double shell, beg shell in same ch-1 sp, ch 3, shell in next ch-1 sp of beg double shell, *ch 3, sk next ch-3 sp, sc in next ch-3 sp, [ch 3, sc in next ch-3 sp] twice, ch 3, sk next ch-3 sp**, [shell in next ch-1 sp of double shell,

CONTINUED ON PAGE 146

Wilbur Worm

BY **MARTHA LOBMEYER**

SKILL LEVEL ■□□□
BEGINNER

FINISHED SIZE
25 inches long

MATERIALS
- Red Heart Super Saver medium (worsted) weight yarn (7 oz/364 yds/198g per skein):
    3 oz each #319 cherry red, #324 bright yellow and #254 pumpkin
    2 oz each #886 blue and #356 amethyst
    ½ oz #312 black
    10 yds #311 white
- Red Heart Kids medium (worsted) weight yarn (5 oz/290 yds/141g per skein):
    2 oz #2652 lime
- Red Heart Classic medium (worsted) weight yarn (3½ oz/190 yds/99g per skein):
    1 skein #245 orange
- Size G/6/4mm crochet hook or size needed to obtain gauge
- Tapestry needle
- Sewing needle and thread
- Fiberfill
- 9 inches ⅞-inch-wide hook-and-loop tape
- Stitch marker

GAUGE
4 sc = 1 inch; 4 sc rnds = 1 inch

PATTERN NOTES
Weave in loose ends as work progresses.

Do not join rounds unless otherwise stated.

Body is crocheted in 9 different segments following rounds of Head as indicated.

Wilbur Worm is not recommended as a toy for children under 3 years of age.

INSTRUCTIONS

EYE
Make 2.
Row 1: With white, work **sc foundation st** *(see Foundation Stitches on page 172)* 6 times, turn. *(6 sc)*

Rows 2–5: Ch 1, sc in each sc across, turn.

Row 6: Ch 1, **sc dec** *(see Stitch Guide)* in next 2 sc, sc in each of next 2 sc, sc dec in next 2 sc, turn. *(4 sc)*

Row 7: Ch 1, [sc dec in next 2 sc] twice, turn. *(2 sc)*

Row 8: Ch 1, sc dec in next 2 sc, **do not turn**. *(1 sc)*

Rnd 9: Now working in rnds, sc evenly sp around, working 3 sc in each corner, join in first sc of row 8. Fasten off.

Pupils
Row 1: With black, work sc foundation st 4 times, turn. *(4 sc)*

Rows 2 & 3: Ch 1, sc in each sc across, turn.

Row 4: [Sc dec in next 2 sc] twice, turn. *(2 sc)*

Row 5: Sc dec in next 2 sc, **do not turn**. *(1 sc)*

Rnd 6: Now working in rnds, sc evenly sp around, working 3 sc in each corner, join in first sc of row 5, leaving a 12-inch length of yarn, fasten off.

Finishing
Sew Pupil to lower right corner of Eye. Attach black to Rnd 9 of Eye on left edge, ch 1, sc in each st around, working 3 sc in each corner st and catching in sts of Pupils that lie along edge of Eye, sl st to join in beg sc, leaving a 12-inch length of yarn, fasten off.

NOSE
Rnd 1: With pumpkin, work **slip ring** *(see Foundation Stitches on page 172)*, work 6 sc

in ring, pull end of yarn to close slip ring. *(6 sc)*

Rnd 2: 2 sc in each sc around. *(12 sc)*

Rnd 3: [Sc in next sc, 2 sc in next sc] around. *(18 sc)*

Rnd 4: [2 sc in next sc, sc in each of next 2 sc] around. *(24 sc)*

Rnd 5: [Sc in each of next 2 sc, sc dec in next 2 sc] around. *(18 sc)*

Rnd 6: [Sc dec in next 2 sc, sc in next sc] around. *(12 sc)*

Stuff nose with fiberfill.

Rnd 7: [Sc dec in next 2 sc] around, sl st in next st, leaving a 6-inch length, fasten off. *(6 sc)*

Weave rem length through sts of rnd 7, pull to close opening, knot to secure.

MOUTH
With black, ch 20, leaving a 12-inch length, fasten off.

[With black, ch 5, leaving 6-inch length, fasten off] twice.

HEAD
Rnd 1: With cherry red, work slip ring, work 6 sc in ring, pull end of yarn to close slip ring. *(6 sc)*

Rnd 2: 2 sc in each sc around. *(12 sc)*

Rnd 3: [Sc in next sc, 2 sc in next sc] around. *(18 sc)*

Rnd 4: [2 sc in next sc, sc in each of next 2 sc] around. *(24 sc)*

Rnd 5: [Sc in each of next 3 sc, 2 sc in next sc] around. *(30 sc)*

Rnd 6: Sc in next sc, 2 sc in next sc, [sc in each of next 4 sc, 2 sc in next sc] 5 times, sc in each of next 3 sc. *(36 sc)*

Rnd 7: [Sc in each of next 5 sc, 2 sc in next sc] around. *(42 sc)*

Rnd 8: Sc in each of next 2 sc, 2 sc in next sc, [sc in each of next 6 sc, 2 sc in next sc] 5 times, sc in each of next 4 sc. *(48 sc)*

Rnd 9: [Sc in each of next 7 sc, 2 sc in next sc] around. *(54 sc)*

Rnd 10: Sc in each of next 3 sc, 2 sc in next sc, [sc in each of next 8 sc, 2 sc in next sc] 5 times, sc in each of next 5 sc. *(60 sc)*

Rnd 11: [Sc in each of next 9 sc, 2 sc in next sc] around. *(66 sc)*

Rnd 12: Sc in each of next 4 sc, 2 sc in next sc, [sc in each of next 10 sc, 2 sc in next sc] 5 times, sc in each of next 6 sc. *(72 sc)*

Rnd 13: [Sc in each of next 11 sc, 2 sc in next sc] around. *(78 sc)*

Rnd 14: Sc in each of next 5 sc, 2 sc in next sc, [sc in each of next 12 sc, 2 sc in next sc] 5 times, sc in each of next 7 sc. *(84 sc)*

Rnd 15: [Sc in each of next 13 sc, 2 sc in next sc] around. *(90 sc)*

Rnd 16: Sc in each sc around.

Rnd 17: Rep rnd 16.

At the end of rnd 17, draw up a lp, remove hook.

Working with tapestry needle and rem lengths of yarns, sew Nose to rnd 1 of Head.

Sew Eyes over rnd 4–15 centered above Nose with ¾-inch sp between.

Sew long Mouth chain centered under Nose over rnd 11, sew short chains at each end of Mouth at slight angle.

Rnd 18: Pick up dropped lp, sc in each of next 6 sc, sc dec in next 2 sc, [sc in each of next 13 sc, sc dec in next 2 sc] 5 times, sc in each of next 7 sc. *(84 sc)*

Rnd 19: [Sc in each of next 12 sc, sc dec in next 2 sc] around. *(78 sc)*

Rnd 20: Sc in each of next 5 sc, sc dec in next 2 sc, [sc in each of next 11 sc, sc dec in next 2 sc] 5 times, sc in each of next 6 sc. *(72 sc)*

Rnd 21: [Sc in each of next 10 sc, sc dec in next 2 sc] around. *(66 sc)*

Rnd 22: Sc in each of next 4 sc, sc dec in next 2 sc, [sc in each of next 9 sc, sc dec in next 2 sc] 5 times, sc in each of next 5 sc. *(60 sc)*

Rnd 23: [Sc in each of next 8 sc, sc dec in next 2 sc] around. *(54 sc)*

Rnd 24: Sc in each of next 3 sc, sc dec in next 2 sc, [sc in each of next 7 sc, sc dec in next 2 sc] 5 times, sc in each of next 4 sc. *(48 sc)*

Rnd 25: [Sc in each of next 6 sc, sc dec in next 2 sc] around. *(42 sc)*

Rnd 26: Sc in each of next 2 sc, sc dec in next 2 sc, [sc in each of next 5 sc, sc dec in next 2 sc] 5 times, sc in each of next 3 sc. *(36 sc)*

Rnd 27: [Sc in each of next 4 sc, sc dec in next 2 sc] around. *(30 sc)*

Rnd 28: Sc in next st, sc dec in next 2 sc, [sc in each of next 3 sc, sc dec in next 2 sc] 5 times, sc in each of next 2 sc. *(24 sc)*

Rnd 29: [Sc in each of next 2 sts, sc dec in next 2 sc] around. *(18 sc)*

Stuff Head with fiberfill slightly flattening. Continue to stuff as work progresses.

Rnd 30: [Sc in next sc, sc dec in next 2 sc] around. *(12 sc)*

Rnd 31: [Sc dec in next 2 sc] around, sl st in next sc, leaving a 6-inch length of yarn, fasten off. *(6 sc)*

Weave yarn through rem sts, pull to close opening, knot to secure.

BODY
First Segment
Rnds 1–14: With bright yellow, rep rnds 1–14 of Head. *(84 sc)*

Rnds 15 & 16: Rep rnd 16 of Head twice.

Rnds 17–29: Rep rnds 19–31 of Head. *(6 sc)*

Second Segment
Rnds 1–13: With pumpkin, rep rnds 1–13 of Head. *(78 sc)*

Rnds 14 & 15: Rep rnd 16 of Head twice.

Rnds 16–27: Rep rnds 20–31 of Head. *(6 sc)*

Third Segment
Rnds 1–12: With blue, rep rnds 1–12 of Head. *(72 sc)*

Rnds 13 & 14: Rep rnd 16 of Head twice.

Rnds 15–25: Rep rnds 21–31 of Head. *(6 sc)*

Fourth Segment
Rnds 1–11: With lime, rep rnds 1–11 of Head. *(66 sc)*

Rnds 12 & 13: Rep rnd 16 of Head twice.

Rnds 14–23: Rep rnds 22–31 of Head. *(6 sc)*

Fifth Segment
Rnds 1–10: With amethyst, rep rnds 1–10 of Head. *(60 sc)*

Rnds 11 & 12: Rep rnd 16 of Head twice.

Rnds 13–21: Rep rnds 23–31 of Head. *(6 sc)*

Sixth Segment
Rnds 1–9: With orange, rep rnds 1–9 of Head. *(54 sc)*

Rnds 10 & 11: Rep rnd 16 of Head twice.

Rnds 12–19: Rep rnds 24–31 of Head. *(6 sc)*

Seventh Segment
Rnds 1–8: With bright yellow, rep rnds 1–8 of Head. *(48 sc)*

Rnds 9 & 10: Rep rnd 16 of Head twice.

Rnds 11–17: Rep rnds 25–31 of Head. *(6 sc)*

Eighth Segment
Rnds 1–7: With cherry red, rep rnds 1–7 of Head. *(42 sc)*

Rnds 8 & 9: Rep rnd 16 of Head twice.

Rnds 10–15: Rep rnds 26–31

of Head. *(6 sc)*

Ninth Segment
Rnds 1–6: With amethyst, rep rnds 1–6 of Head. *(36 sc)*

Rnds 7 & 8: Rep rnd 16 of Head twice.

Rnds 9–13: Rep rnds 27–31 of Head. *(6 sc)*

FINISHING
With hook-and-loop tape sections tog, cut tape into 9 equal sections; round off corners of each section with scissors.

Pull sections apart. Sew first piece to center of back of Head, sew 2nd piece of same section to center of rnd 1 of first Body Segment.

[Pull next section apart. Sew first piece to center back of last rnd of same segment; sew 2nd piece of same section to center of rnd 1 of next Body Segment] rep until all hook-and-loop tape sections are used, joining segments tog in order of size as work progresses. ●

Pocket Bibs CONTINUED FROM PAGE 115

Join rounds with slip stitch unless otherwise stated.

SPECIAL STITCHES
Shell: 5 dc in indicated sc.

Beginning shell (beg shell): Ch 3, 4 dc in same sc.

Increase shell (inc shell): Ch 4, 4 dc in 4th ch from hook.

INSTRUCTIONS

BIB
Row 1: Starting at neckline edge with lime, work **sc foundation st** *(see Foundation*

Stitches on page 172) 19 times, turn. *(19 sc)*

Row 2: Beg shell *(see Special Stitches)* in first sc, [sk next 2 sc, sc in next sc, sk next 2 sc, **shell** *(see Special Stitches)* in next sc] 3 times, turn. *(4 shells, 3 sc)*

Row 3: Inc shell *(see Special Stitches)*, [sk next 2 dc, sc in next dc, sk next 2 dc, shell in next sc] 3 times, sk next 2 dc, sc in next dc, sk next dc, shell in last dc, turn. *(5 shells, 4 sc)*

Row 4: Inc shell, [sk next 2 dc, sc in next dc, sk next 2 dc, shell in next sc] 4 times, sk next 2 dc, sc in next dc, sk next dc, shell in last dc, turn. *(6 shells, 5 sc)*

Row 5: Ch 3 *(counts as first dc)*, 2 dc in same st, sk 1 dc, [sc in next dc, sk next 2 dc, shell in next sc,

sk next 2 dc] 5 times, sc in next dc, sk next dc, 3 dc in last dc, turn. *(5 shells, 6 sc, 2 half shells)*

Row 6: Ch 1, sc in same st as beg ch-1, [sk next 2 dc, shell in next sc, sk next 2 dc, sc in next dc] 5 times, shell in next sc, sk next 2 dc, sc in next dc.

Row 7: Ch 3, 2 dc in same st as beg ch-3, sk next 2 dc, [sc in next dc, sk next 2 dc, shell in next sc, sk next 2 dc] 5 times, sc in next dc, sk next 2 dc, 3 dc in last sc, turn. *(5 shells, 6 sc, 2 half shells)*

Rows 8–33: [Rep rows 6 and 7 alternately] 13 times. At the end of last rep, fasten off.

Row 34: Attach snow with sl st in first st of row 33, ch 1, sc in same sc as beg ch-1, sc in each of next 2 sc, [sl st in next sc, sc in each of

next 5 dc] 5 times, sl st in next sc, sc in each of next 3 dc. Fasten off.

Fold row 30–34 upward and secure with straight pins.

EDGING

Row 1 (RS): Attach snow in right bottom corner with sl st, ch 1, working through both thicknesses, work 7 sc up folded edge, sc in side edge of each row to row 1, *[work sc foundation st] 49 times *(first tie)*, ch 1, working in opposite side of foundation, sc in each of next 49 sts*, sc in opposite side of foundation across neckline, rep from * to * for 2nd tie, sc evenly sp down opposite edge of Bib to folded section, working through both thicknesses, work 7 sc across edge. Fasten off.

Remove straight pins. ●

Autumn Rose Hat CONTINUED FROM PAGE 121

ROSE
Rnd 1 (WS): With size F hook and jockey red, leaving 12-inch length at beg, work slip ring, ch 1, [sc in slip ring, ch 3] 4 times,

join *(see Pattern Notes)* in beg sc. *(4 ch-3 sps)*

Rnd 2: Ch 1, (sc, 5 dc, sc) in each ch-3 sp around, join in beg sc. *(4 petals)*

Rnd 3: Ch 1, working in front of petals, **fpsc** *(see Stitch Guide)* around first sc on rnd 1, ch 3, [fpsc around next sc on rnd 1, ch 3] 3 times, join in beg sc. *(4 ch-3 sps)*

Rnd 4: Ch 1, (sc, 5 tr, sc) in each ch-3 sp around, join in beg sc. *(4 petals)*

Rnd 5: Ch 1, working in front of petals, fpsc around first sc on rnd 3, ch 8, [fpsc around next sc on rnd 3, ch 8] 3 times, join in beg sc. *(4 ch-8 sps)*

Rnd 6: Ch 1, (sc, 7 tr, sc, 7 tr, sc) in each ch-8 sp around, join in beg sc. *(4 double petals)*

Rnd 7: Ch 1, working in front of petals, fpsc around first sc on rnd 5, ch 5, fpsc around 2nd sc on rnd 5, ch 5, fpsc around 3rd sc on rnd 5, fasten off. *(2 ch-5 sps)*

LEAVES
Row 1: With size F hook, join

paddy green with sl st in ch-5 sp, ch 3, 7 dc in same sp, turn. *(8 dc)*

Row 2: Ch 3, **dc dec** *(see Stitch Guide)* in next 2 sts, dc in each of next 2 sts, dc dec in next 2 sts, dc in last st, turn. *(6 dc)*

Row 3: Ch 3, [dc dec in next 2 sts] twice, dc in last st, turn. *(4 dc)*

Row 4: Ch 3, **3-dc cl** *(see Special Stitch)* in next 3 dc, fasten off.

Join paddy green in next ch-5 sp, rep rows 1–4.

FINISHING
Thread tapestry needle with jockey red. Draw first petal made to center of Rose; tack in place to form center bud. Fold 1 side of Hat brim up along rnd 10. Bring yarn end to center back of Rose; tack Rose to Hat. ●

T-Strap Booties CONTINUED FROM PAGE 122

sk 10 sts from where Sole was fastened off, attach yarn with sl st in next st, ch 2, hdc in each of next 19 sts, turn. *(20 hdc)*

Row 2: Ch 2, [**hdc dec** *(see Stitch Guide)* in next 2 sts] 9 times, hdc in last st, turn. *(11 hdc)*

Row 3: Ch 1, [**sc dec** *(see Stitch Guide)* in next 2 sts] 5 times, leaving last unworked, turn. *(5 sc)*

Row 4: Ch 1, [sc dec in next 2 sts] twice, sc in last st, turn. *(3 sc)*

Rows 5–17: Ch 1, sc in each of next 3 sts, turn. At the end of row 17, leaving 7-inch length of yarn, fasten off. Fold row 17 under and sew to row 8.

RIGHT BOOTIE STRAP
Row 1 (RS): Attach yarn with sl st in 5th st to the right of joining st on back of heel, ch 1, sc in same st as beg ch-1, sc in each of next 10 sts, turn. *(11 sc)*

Row 2: Ch 16, sc in 2nd ch from hook, sc in each of next 14 chs, sc in each of next 11 sc, turn. *(26 sc)*

Row 3: Ch 1, sc in each of next 26 sc, ch 4, sl st in end ch at bottom of row 2 *(button lp)*, fasten off.

LEFT BOOTIE STRAP
Row 1 (RS): Attach yarn with sl st in 7th st to the left of joining on back of heel, ch 1, sc in same st as beg ch-1, sc in each of next 10 sts, turn. *(11 sc)*

Rows 2 & 3: Rep rows 2 and 3 of Right Bootie Strap.

FINISHING
Sew a button to each Bootie at edge of row 3, pass strap through pocket at center of Upper Toe, insert button into button lp on Bootie. ●

Spiral Popcorn Baby Blanket CONTINUED FROM PAGE 126

just made, dc in next st, **pc** *(see Special Stitch)* in next st, 2 dc in next st, [dc in each of next 2 sts, pc in next st, 2 dc in next st] twice, draw up 4-inch lp, drop lp from hook, *pick up dropped lp of next color, tighten lp around hook, [dc in each of

next 2 sts, pc in next st, 2 dc in next st] 3 times, draw up 4-inch lp, remove lp from hook, rep from * twice. *(48 dc, 12 pc)*

Rnds 6–19: Pick up next dropped C lp, tighten lp around hook, dc in first st of next color, mark st just made, dc in each st across to next pc, dc in next pc, sk ch-1 sp at top of pc, pc in next st, 2 dc in next st, [dc in each st across to next pc, dc in next pc, sk ch-1 at top of pc, pc in next st, 2 dc in next st] twice, draw up 4-inch lp, drop lp from hook, *pick up dropped lp of next color, tighten lp around hook, [dc in each st across to next pc, dc in next pc, sk ch-1 sp at top of pc, pc in next st, 2 dc in next st] 3 times, draw up 4-inch lp, drop lp from hook,

rep from * twice. (204 dc, 12 pc at end of last rnd)

ENDING SPIRALS
Rnd 20: Pick up next dropped C lp, tighten lp around hook, hdc in first st of next color, hdc in each of next 2 sts, sc in each of next 3 sts, sl st in each of next 3 sts, fasten off C, [pick up dropped lp of next color, tighten lp around hook, hdc in each of next 3 sts, sc in each of next 3 sts, sl st in each of next 3 sts, fasten off] around, **do not**

fasten off last color A lp.

RUFFLE
Rnd 21: Ch 3, 2 dc in same st as beg ch-3, 3 dc in each st around, sl st to join in 3rd ch of ch-3. (648 dc)

Rnd 22: Ch 3, dc in each st around, join with sl st to in 3rd ch of ch-3. Fasten off.

Rnd 23: Join B with sl st in any st, ch 1, sc in each st around, sl st to join in first sc. Fasten off. ●

Little Garden Coat CONTINUED FROM PAGE 133

Row 6: Ch 2, [sc in next dc, dc in next sc] 10 [11, 12] times, turn.

Rows 7 & 8: Rep rows 5 and 6.

Row 9: Ch 2, sc in same st as beg ch-2, [sc in next sc, sc in next dc] 10 [11, 12] times, dc in same st as last sc, turn. (23 [25, 27] sts)

Row 10: Ch 1, sc in same st, [dc in next sc, sc in next dc] 11 [12, 13] times, turn.

Row 11: Ch 2, [sc in next dc, dc in next sc] 11 [12, 13] times, turn.

Row 12: Rep row 10.

Row 13: Rep row 11.

Row 14: Ch 2, sc in same st as beg ch-2, [dc in next sc, sc in next dc] 11 [12, 13] times, dc in same st as last sc, turn. (25 [27, 29] sts)

Row 15: Ch 1, sc in same st, [dc in next sc, sc in next dc] 12 [13, 14] times, turn.

Row 16: Ch 2, [sc in next dc, dc in next sc] 12 [13, 14] times, turn.

For Size 12–18 Months Only
Rep rows [15 and 16] once.

For Size 18–24 Months Only
Next rows: Rep row [15] twice.

Next rows: Rep row [16] twice.

For All Sizes
Row 17: Ch 1, sk first st, [dc in next sc, sc in next dc] 11 [12, 13] times, dc in next sc, leaving rem st unworked, turn. (23 [25, 27] sts)

Row 18: Ch 1, sk first st, dc in next sc, [sc in next dc, dc in next sc] 10 [11, 12] times,

leaving rem st unworked, turn. (21 [23, 25] sts)

Row 19: Sk first st, sl st in next 2 sts, ch 1, beg in same st as ch-1, [sc in next dc, dc in next sc] 8 [9, 10] times, sc in next dc, leaving rem sts unworked, turn. (17 [19, 21] sts)

Row 20: Sk first st, ch 1, [sc in next dc, dc in next sc] 7 [8, 9] times, sc in next dc, leaving rem st unworked, turn. (15 [17, 19] sts)

Fasten off sizes 6–12 months and 12–18 months.

For Size 18–24 Months Only

Row [21]: Sk first st, ch 1, [dc in next sc, sc in next dc] [8] times, dc in next sc, leaving rem st unworked, turn. *([17] sts)*

Row [22]: Sk first st, ch 1, [dc in next sc, sc in next dc] [7] times, dc in next sc, leaving rem st unworked, turn. Fasten off. *([15] sts)*

For All Sizes

Sew Sleeve seam.

SLEEVE CUFF

Rnd 1: With RS facing, attach B with sl st in Sleeve seam, ch 1, sc in each st around, **join** *(see Pattern Notes)* in beg sc, **do not turn**. *(19 [21, 23] sc)*

Rnds 2 & 3: Ch 1, sc in each sc around, join in beg sc. At the end of rnd 3, fasten off.

ASSEMBLY

With WS facing, sew shoulder seams and sew Sleeves into armhole opening.

LEFT BUTTONHOLE BAND

Row 1: With RS facing, attach B with sl st at top in neckline edge, ch 1, sc evenly sp down to bottom edge, turn.

Row 2: Ch 1, sc in each sc across, turn.

Row 3: Ch 1, sc in same st, sc in next st, [ch 2, sk next 2 sts, sc in each of next 7 sts] twice, ch 2, sk next 2 sts, sc in each sc to bottom edge, turn. *(3 buttonholes)*

Row 4: Ch 1, sc in each st across to next ch-2 sp, [2 sc in next ch-2 sp, sc in each of next 7 sc] twice, 2 sc in next ch-2 sp, sc in each of next 2 sc, turn.

Row 5: Rep row 2. Fasten off.

RIGHT BUTTON BAND

Row 1: With RS facing, attach B with sl st to bottom corner, ch 1, sc evenly sp up front edge to neckline edge, turn.

Rows 2–5: Ch 1, sc in each sc across, turn. At the end of row 5, fasten off.

COLLAR

Row 1: With RS facing, attach B with sl st in row 1 of Right Button Band, ch 1, sc in same st as beg ch-1, sc evenly sp around neckline, sc in side edge of row 1 of Left Button-hole Band, turn.

Row 2: Ch 1, 2 sc in first sc, sc in each sc across to last sc, 2 sc in last sc, turn.

Row 3: Rep row 2.

Row 4: Ch 1, sc in each sc across, turn.

Rows 5–7 [5–7, 5–8]: Rep row 4. At the end of last rep, fasten off.

Row 8 [8, 9]: With RS facing, attach C in side edge of row 1 of Collar, ch 1, sc in same st as beg ch-1, sc in side edge of each row to corner, 3 sc in corner st, sc in each sc across Collar, 3 sc in corner st, sc in side edge of each rem row of Collar. Fasten off.

POCKET
Make 2.

Rnd 1: With C, work **slip ring** *(see Foundation Stitches page 172)*, ch 1, 10 sc in slip ring. Fasten off. *(10 sc)*

Rnd 2: Attach B with sl st in any sc of rnd 1, ch 1, (sc, hdc, ch 1, dc, ch 1, hdc, sc) in same st as beg ch-1, sk next st, [(sc, hdc, ch 1, dc, ch 1, hdc, sc) in next sc, sk next sc] 4 times, join in first sc. Fasten off. *(5 petals)*

Rnd 3: Attach A with sl st between any two sc of rnd 2, holding Petals forward and keeping ch lps behind petals, [ch 3, sl st between next 2 sc of rnd 2] 4 times, ch 3, sl st in same st as joining. *(5 ch-3 lps)*

Rnd 4: Sl st into ch-3 sp, ch 3 *(counts as first dc)*, 4 dc in same ch-3 sp, [5 dc in next ch-3 sp] 4 times, join in 3rd ch of ch-3. *(25 dc)*

Row 5: Now working in rows, working across top edge of Pocket, ch 2, dc in next st, **hdc dec** *(see Stitch Guide)* in next 2 sts, sc in each of next 3 sts, hdc dec in next 2 sts, dc in next st, ch 2, sl st in next st. Fasten off. *(9 sts)*

Rnd 6: Now working in rnds, attach C to last ch-2 sp of row 5, ch 1, 2 sc in ch-2 sp, sc in each st to next ch-2 sp, 2 sc in ch-2 sp, sc in each st across top edge of Pocket, join in beg sc. Fasten off.

Sew Pocket centered to each front bottom 1 inch above bottom edge of Coat. ●

Peekins Summer Dress CONTINUED FROM PAGE 137

next shell, ch 4, sk next ch-3 sp, sc in next ch-3 sp, ch 4, sk next ch-3 sp**, shell in ch-1 sp of next shell, rep from * around, ending last rep at **, join in 3rd ch of beg ch-3.

Rnd 9: Sl st in ch-1 sp of beg shell, beg shell in same ch-1 sp, *ch 3, sk next ch-3 sp, dc in next dc, [ch 3, dc in next dc] 6 times, ch 3, sk next ch-3 sp**, [shell in ch-1 sp of next shell] twice, rep from * around, ending last rep at **, shell in ch-1 sp of next shell, join in 3rd ch of beg ch-3.

Rnd 10: Sl st in ch-1 sp of beg shell, beg shell in same ch-1 sp, *ch 3, sk next ch-3 sp, sc in next ch-3 sp, [ch 3, sc in next ch-3 sp] 5 times, ch 3, sk next ch-3 sp**, [shell in ch-1 sp of next shell] twice, rep from * around, ending last rep at **, shell in ch-1 sp of next shell, join in 3rd ch of beg ch-3.

Rnd 11: Sl st in ch-1 sp of beg shell, beg shell in same ch-1 sp, *ch 3, sk next ch-3 sp, sc in next ch-3 sp, [ch 3, sc in next ch-3 sp] 4 times, ch 3, sk next ch-3 sp, shell in ch-1 sp of next shell, ch 3**, shell in ch-1 sp of next shell, rep from * around, ending last rep at **, join in 3rd ch of beg ch-3.

Rnd 12: Sl st in ch-1 sp of beg shell, beg shell in same ch-1 sp, *ch 3, sk next ch-3 sp, sc in next ch-3 sp, [ch 3, sc in next ch-3 sp] 3 times, ch 3, sk next ch-3 sp, shell in ch-1 sp of next shell, ch 3, V-st in next ch-3 sp, ch 3**,

ch 3] twice, rep from * around, ending last rep at **, join in 3rd ch of beg ch-3.

Rnd 7: Sl st in ch-1 sp of beg double shell, beg shell in same ch-1 sp, ch 3, V-st in next ch-3 sp, ch 3, shell in ch-1 sp of next shell, *ch 3, sk next ch-3 sp, [sc in next ch-3 sp, ch 3] twice, sk next ch-3 sp**, shell in ch-1 sp of next shell, ch 3, V-st in next ch-3 sp, ch 3, shell in ch-1 sp of next shell, rep from * around, ending last rep at **, join in 3rd ch of beg ch-3.

Rnd 8: Sl st in ch-1 sp of beg shell, beg shell in same ch-1 sp, *ch 3, sk next ch-3 sp, 7 dc in ch-1 sp of next V-st, ch 3, sk next ch-3 sp, shell in ch-1 sp of

shell in ch-1 sp of next shell, rep from * around, ending last rep at **, join in 3rd ch of beg ch-3.

Rnd 13: Sl st in ch-1 sp of beg shell, beg shell in same ch-1 sp, *ch 3, sk next ch-3 sp, sc in next ch-3 sp, [ch 3, sc in next ch-3 sp] twice, ch 3, sk next ch-3 sp, shell in ch-1 sp of next shell, ch 3, 7 dc in ch-1 sp of next V-st, ch 3, sk next ch-3 sp**, shell in ch-1 sp of next shell, rep from * around, ending last rep at **, join in 3rd ch of beg ch-3.

Rnd 14: Sl st in ch-1 sp of beg shell, beg shell in same ch-1 sp, *ch 3, sk next ch-3 sp, [sc in next ch-3 sp, ch 3] twice, sk next ch-3 sp, shell in ch-1 sp of next shell, ch 3, sk next ch-3 sp, dc in first dc of 7-dc group, [ch 3, dc in next dc] 6 times, ch 3, sk next ch-3 sp**, shell in ch-1 sp of next shell, rep from * around, ending last rep at **, join in 3rd ch of beg ch-3.

Rnd 15: Sl st in ch-1 sp of beg shell, beg shell in same ch-1 sp, *ch 4, sk next ch-3 sp, sc in next ch-3 sp, ch 4, sk next ch-3 sp, shell in ch-1 sp of next shell, ch 3, sk next ch-3 sp, sc in next ch-3 sp, [ch 3, sc in next ch-3 sp] 5 times, ch 3, sk next ch-3 sp**, shell in ch-1 sp of next shell, rep from * around, ending last rep at **, join in 3rd ch of beg ch-3.

Rnd 16: Sl st in ch-1 sp of beg shell, beg shell in same ch-1 sp, *sk next ch-4 sp, sk next sc, sk next ch-4 sp, shell in ch-1 sp of next shell, ch 4, sk next ch-3 sp, sc in next ch-3 sp, [ch 3, sc in next ch-3 sp] 4 times, ch 4, sk next ch-3 sp**, shell in ch-1 sp of next shell, rep from * around, ending last rep at **, join in 3rd ch of beg ch-3.

Rnd 17: Sl st in ch-1 sp of beg shell, beg shell in same ch-1 sp, *ch 3, shell in ch-1 sp of next shell, ch 4, sc in next ch-3 sp, [ch 3, sc in next ch-3 sp] 3 times, ch 4**, shell in ch-1 sp of next shell, rep from * around, ending last rep at **, join in 3rd ch of beg ch-3.

Rnd 18: Sl st in ch-1 sp of beg shell, beg shell in same ch-1 sp, *ch 3, V-st in ch-3 sp, ch 3, shell in ch-1 sp of next shell, ch 4, sc in next ch-3 sp, [ch 3, sc in next ch-3 sp] twice, ch 4**, shell in ch-1 sp of next shell, rep from * around, ending last rep at **, join in 3rd ch of beg ch-3.

Rnd 19: Sl st in ch-1 sp of beg shell, beg shell in same ch-1 sp, *ch 3, V-st in next ch-3 sp, ch 3, sk next V-st, V-st in next ch-3 sp, ch 3, shell in ch-1 sp of next shell, ch 4, sc in next ch-3 sp, ch 3, sc in next ch-3 sp, ch 4**, shell in ch-1 sp of next shell, rep from * around, ending last rep at **, join in 3rd ch of beg ch-3.

Rnd 20: Sl st in ch-1 sp of beg shell, beg shell in same ch-1 sp, *[ch 3, V-st in next ch-3 sp] 3 times, ch 3, shell in ch-1 sp of next shell, ch 4, sc in next ch-3 sp, ch 4**, shell in ch-1 sp of next shell, rep from * around, join in 3rd ch of beg ch-3.

Rnd 21: Sl st in ch-1 sp of beg shell, ch 3, dc, **picot** (see Special Stitches), 2 dc in ch-1 sp of next shell, *[ch 3, **picot shell** (see Special Stitches) in next ch-3 sp] 4 times, ch 3, picot shell in ch-1 sp of next shell, ch 2, sc in next sc, ch 2**, picot shell ch-1 sp of in next shell, rep from * around, ending last rep at **, join in 3rd ch of beg ch-3. Fasten off.

SHOULDER SHAPING
Make 2.
Rnd 1 (RS): Join natural with sl st in center ch-1 sp at underarm, ch 1, work 45 sc evenly sp around armhole opening, join in beg sc, **do not turn**.

Note: Do not use center 4 sc of underarm, these sts will be skipped.

Row 2: Now working in rows, leaving 4 underarm sts free, sl st in next sc of rnd 1, ch 1, sc in same sc, ch 4, sk next 4 sc, shell in next sc, *ch 2, sk next 4 sc, 5 dc in next sc, ch 2, sk next 4 sc, shell in next sc, rep from * twice, ch 4, sk next 4 sc, sc in next sc, turn. *(4 shells, 3 pineapple bases)*

Row 3: Ch 5, sk ch-4 sp, *shell in ch-1 sp of next shell, ch 2, sk next ch-2 sp, dc in first dc of 5-dc group, [ch 3, dc in next dc] 4 times, ch 2, sk next ch-2 sp, rep from * twice, shell in ch-1 sp of next shell, ch 5, sk next ch-4 sp, sl st in next sc, turn.

Row 4: Ch 5, sk next ch-5 sp, *shell in ch-1 sp of next shell, ch 3, sk next ch-2 sp, sc in next ch-3 sp, [ch 3, sc in next ch-3 sp] 3 times, ch 3, rep from * twice, shell in ch-1 sp of next shell, sk next ch-5 sp, dtr in next sl st, turn.

Row 5: Sl st in ch-1 sp of next shell, *ch 3, sk next ch-3 sp, sc in next ch-3 sp, [ch 3, sc in next ch-3 sp] twice, ch 3**, shell in ch-1 sp of next shell, rep from * from twice, ending last rep at **, sl st in ch-1 sp of last shell, turn.

Row 6: Picot in ch-1 sp, sl st in each of next 3 chs, sl st in first ch-3 sp of pineapple, *ch 4, sl st in 3rd ch from hook, ch 1, sc in next ch-3 sp, ch 4, picot shell in next shell, ch 4, sc in next ch-3 sp, rep from * once, ch 4, sl st in 3rd ch from hook, ch 1, sc in next ch-3 sp, sl st across rem chs to next ch-1 sp of last shell, picot in same shell sp. Fasten off.

RIGHT BACK OPENING
Row 1: With WS facing, beg at bottom waistline, ch 1, sc evenly sp across Back Opening, turn.

Row 2: Ch 1, sc in each sc across. Fasten off.

LEFT BACK OPENING
Row 1: With RS facing, beg at bottom waistline, join natural with sl st, ch 1, sc evenly sp across Back Opening, turn.

Row 2: Ch 1, sc in each sc across, working [ch 2, sk next 2 sc for each buttonhole] 4 times evenly across back opening.

Fasten off.

Sew buttons to Right Back opposite buttonholes. ●

Two Skeins or Less

Chapter Contents